CoderDojo
<NANO>

CREATE WITH <CODE>

BUILD YOUR OWN WEBSITE

‹ABOUT CODERDOJO›

This book is about coding. Maybe the first steps you'll take towards becoming a seriously good coder. And, if you're interested in coding, you may have heard of CoderDojo.

CoderDojo is a coding club for young people which lets you hang out with other coders, learn new stuff and generally have fun with computers. It's free and you work with your friends. If you're lucky, there's a Dojo near you. Maybe you've been down and done some coding? But maybe there isn't – or maybe you just want to do even more coding?

If so, don't worry. You can just get your own official mini-Dojo, a Dojo Nano, up and running. How? It's easy.

Ingredients for a Dojo Nano:

- ☯ **one or more friends**
- ☯ **a computer**
- ☯ **this book**

WHAT'S A DOJO NANO?

What happens at your Dojo Nano? Basically, whatever you think is cool coding-wise. In this book we're going to meet the Nanonauts, who have set up their own Dojo Nano where they will be learning to make a website for their band. They'll be combining HTML, CSS and JavaScript to make their website, and you can learn these skills to make your own website as well!

IDEAS + FRIENDS + CODE = DOJO NANO

As a start, with the help of this book, you're going to make your Dojo Nano website, and then maybe a couple of sites for your friends. It's easy, it's fun, and this book will set you on the way! You can follow along with building the site at http://nano.tips, and find more about CoderDojo at http://coderdojo.com

‹INTRODUCING THE NANONAUTS›

Holly, Dervla, Daniel and Sam are in a band called the Nanonauts. Holly plays guitar, Dervla piano, Daniel sings and Sam plays bass. They've started to play quite a few concerts and think it would be great if they could build a website to tell the world about their music.

As soon as the Nanonauts start talking about it they had loads of ideas for their site –

- we could tell people when we were playing our next concert
- we could advertise our CD and T-shirt
- we could have links to our YouTube videos
- we could have tips on buying instruments – and taking care of them
- we could have tips on practising without driving the neighbours crazy

… which they eventually turn into this **site map**:

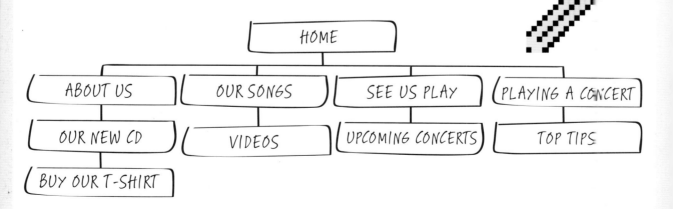

In this book, we'll start to build the site that the Nanonauts sketched in their site map. If you want to, you can follow the examples and build a site about the Nanonauts. But if you have your own band, or want to make the pages about something completely different, that's fine too! Just get stuck into the code and don't be afraid to experiment. If something doesn't work at first, don't get disheartened. Look at your code carefully and see if you can spot where it's not working. Programmers call that 'debugging'.

Read on to find out how to turn Holly's site map into a real website!

THINGS TO DO NEXT

Why not sketch out a site map of your own for a website that you'd like to make? If you don't want to make one about a band, here are some ideas:
- a site about your pets
- a site about your favourite games
- a site about your school friends
- a site about your hobby
- a site about things to do in your town

NINJA TIP

All of the pages you will make in this book are online. You can follow along as the Nanonauts build their website, and copy the code to save time. For more information, go to http://nano.tips/examples

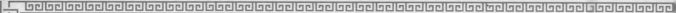

‹ABOUT US› EDITING YOUR FIRST WEB PAGE

So, let's get going! This is the code for a simple web page:

1. Type this code into a simple **plain-text editor** such as Notepad (Windows), GEdit (Ubuntu) or in a **code editor** such as Brackets, Notepad++ or Atom. If you're not sure how to do this go to http://nano.tips/texteditors

```
<!DOCTYPE html>
<html>
<head>
<title>About Us</title>
</head>
<body>
<h1>About Us</h1>
<p>We are the Nanonauts.</p>
<p>Our names are Holly, Dervla, Daniel and Sam.</p>
</body>
</html>
```

```
• index.html (Getting Started) — Brackets

Working Files        ⚙ ⊞        1    <!DOCTYPE html>
                                 2  ▽ <html>
• index.html                    3  ▽ <head>
                                 4    <title>About Us</title>
                                 5    </head>
Getting Started ▾               6  ▽ <body>
                                 7    <h1>About Us</h1>
  index.html                    8    <p>We are the Nanonauts.</p>
  ▸ screenshots                 9    <p>Our names are Holly, Dervla, Daniel and Sam.</p>
                                10    </body>
                                11    </html>



Line 11, Column 8 — 11 Lines                                    INS    HTML ▾         Spaces: 4
```

NINJA TIP

Don't try to edit your pages in a word processor such as Microsoft Word or LibreOffice.

NINJA TIP

about-us.html is the **file name** of the web page. The **.html** bit is called the **file extension**. This tells the various programs of your computer that **about-us.html** is a web page.

Sometimes file extensions get hidden in Windows so that you only see **about-us** rather than **about-us.html**. This can be confusing so make sure that they are visible – if you're not sure how to do this, go to http://nano.tips/findfiles

2. Next, make a folder on your computer called **nanonauts** and save the code as a file called **about-us.html**.

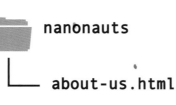

nanonauts

about-us.html

3. The code tells a **web browser**, such as Chrome or Firefox, what is in the webpage. This type of code is known as **HTML**, which stands for Hypertext Markup Language.

Let's open the file in our web browser. This time, instead of looking at the code, you'll see the web page as it is meant to be seen! You can usually do this just by clicking or double-clicking the file – if you're having trouble, go to http://nano.tips/openfiles

About Us

We are the Nanonauts.

Our names are Holly, Dervla, Daniel and Sam.

CHANGE IT!

4. Now you have the same file open in your web browser and the code editor. Arrange the windows so that you can see the code editor and the web browser at the same time.

Change the text in the code editor so that it shows the names of you and your friends. Change the name of the band if you like as well. So instead of saying 'Our names are Holly, Dervla, Daniel and Sam.' it might say 'Our names are 'Anna, Ali, Zeke and Zoe'. To change the text, click in the code editor and type in the new text. Don't change the **tags** – the things between the **angle brackets** such as **<h1>** and **<p>** – just change the text between them.

NINJA TIP

When you're developing a website you'll need to open the web pages in two different applications:
- ☯ a plain-text editor or a code editor to write the code for the page
- ☯ a web browser to see the results

This can be a little confusing at first, but you'll soon get used to it!

‹ADD A STYLESHEET›

We're now going to change how the page looks. To do this we're going to create a **stylesheet**. A stylesheet tells you how the web page should look. Should the background be white or blue or green? Should the text be large or small? Should the links change colour when you roll the mouse over them?

The stylesheet is the place where you keep all this information. The stylesheet is kept separate from the **.html** file so that you can change the web page's colour scheme without having to change the HTML code of the page itself.

1. The stylesheet we'll be creating will be in a new file called **my-first-stylesheet.css**. Notice that the file extension of the stylesheet is **.css** not **.html**. (Stylesheets in this book will be orange, so that you can tell the difference at a glance.) To keep things neat we'll save our stylesheet in its own folder. We'll name this folder **css** and create it inside the **nanonauts** folder.

2. Type in the code from the orange box and save it as **my-first-stylesheet.css** in the **css** folder.

```css
body {
font-family: sans-serif;
}
```

3. To link the stylesheet to the web page, you need to add an extra line into your HTML – it's highlighted in the code below.

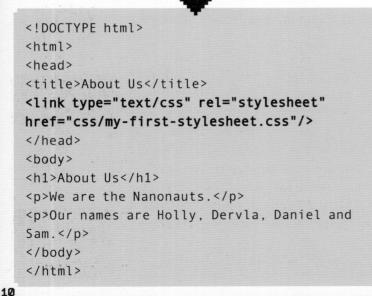

```html
<!DOCTYPE html>
<html>
<head>
<title>About Us</title>
<link type="text/css" rel="stylesheet"
href="css/my-first-stylesheet.css"/>
</head>
<body>
<h1>About Us</h1>
<p>We are the Nanonauts.</p>
<p>Our names are Holly, Dervla, Daniel and
Sam.</p>
</body>
</html>
```

4. What this line does is link the web page to the stylesheet called **my-first-stylesheet.css**.

This stylesheet is kept in the **css** folder (that's what the line of code **css/my-first-stylesheet.css** refers to!) In other words the stylesheet you've just created.

To see the difference the stylesheet makes to the web page, you must reload the page. To reload the page, click on the Reload symbol in the toolbar.

5. After it's reloaded, the page looks a little different. That's because the words are now displaying in a **sans-serif** font – that's what **font-family: sans-serif;** does in the stylesheet.

A **serif** font looks like this

A **sans-serif** font looks like this

About Us

We are the Nanonauts.

Our names are Holly, Dervla, Daniel and Sam.

About Us

We are the Nanonauts.

Our names are Holly, Dervla, Daniel and Sam.

CONGRATULATIONS!

YOU'VE MADE A WEB PAGE AND A STYLESHEET – AND THEY'RE WORKING TOGETHER!

THINGS TO DO NEXT

Enter some more paragraphs of text. Paragraphs go between the **<p>** and **</p>** tags. Like this:

```
<p>I am learning how to make a website for my Dojo
Nano.</p>
```

<p> is a start tag. **</p>** is an end tag. Can you spot the difference?

You can see now that a web page is just text typed into a text file. How the text appears on the web page is controlled by the tags. What happens if you use **h1** or **h2** tags instead of **p** tags? What happens if you put some words inside **strong**?

Like this: `<p>My name is <strong>Sam</strong></p>`

BADGE UNLOCKED

HELLO WORLD!

WORDS TO REMEMBER

Code editor – a program that allows you to edit the HTML code for your web page. You don't have to use a special code editor – Notepad will do just fine – but code editors make it easier by colour-coding the HTML markup and providing other helpful features.

Edit – when you make changes to a web page, you edit it.

File – whenever you save anything onto your computer or up to the web, it's stored as a file. Files can contain any kind of information – they can be web pages, photos, songs, PDF documents, you name it. But programmers refer to all of these things as files.

File name – files always have a file name. So the About Us web page has a file name: **about-us.html**. File names usually end with a full-stop followed by three or four letters (such as **.jpg**, **.pdf**, **.html**). This is known as a **file extension** and it tells the computer what kind of file it is. For example, a file ending **.jpg** is an image file.

Folder – when you save a file, it goes into a folder. A folder is a particular storage location on a computer. Folders can contain other folders. You refer to a folder by giving its **path**. For example, **C:/nanonauts/images** gives the path to the **images** folder inside the **nanonauts** folder on your computer's **C:** drive.

Tags – are special markers used in HTML code. They use angle brackets and look like these examples: **<p> </p> <h1> </h1>
**. You'll be seeing a lot more of them throughout this book!

Web browser – Chrome, Firefox, Internet Explorer, Opera, Safari and other applications which let you browse the web are called web browsers. To view a web page you need a web browser.

NINJA TIP

Some word-processing programs will automatically turn your quote marks (") into 'smart quotes' (","). Your code won't work! Use a plain-text editor.

MORE ONLINE

Want to know more about editing code using a code editor? Go to http://nano.tips/codeeditor

ADDING A PHOTO TO THE PAGE

The About Us page tells everyone about the band. But wouldn't it be more interesting if it showed a photo as well? To show a photo you've got to tell the web browser where to find it. And to understand where to look, the web browser needs to know **1.** the name of the folder in which the photo is stored and **2.** the file name of the picture. Let's say you have a picture called '**nanonauts.jpg**'.

You can add the picture to the page by adding the following line of code:

```
<p><img src="images/nanonauts.jpg"
alt="Picture of the Nanonauts"/></p>
```

This is how the modified code looks:

```
<!DOCTYPE html>
<html>
<head>
<title>About Us</title>
<link type="text/css" rel="stylesheet"
href="css/my-first-stylesheet.css"/>
</head>
<body>
<h1>About Us</h1>
<p><img src="images/nanonauts.jpg"
alt="Picture of the Nanonauts"/></p>
<p>We are the Nanonauts.</p>
<p>Our names are Holly, Dervla, Daniel and
Sam.</p>
</body>
</html>
```

After saving the page and reloading it in the browser, it looks like this:

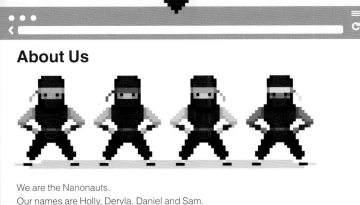

About Us

We are the Nanonauts.
Our names are Holly, Dervla, Daniel and Sam.

Let's take a closer look at the code.

```
<p><img src="images/nanonauts.jpg" alt="Picture of the Nanonauts" /></p>
```

The really important part here is **src="images/nanonauts.jpg"**

This tells the web browser to look inside the **images** folder for a file named **nanonauts.jpg**. The web browser looks for the **images** folder in the same place that the web page is saved. So, if you look at the files in the **nanonauts** folder, as well as the **about-us.html** file, you'll see an **images** folder. And, if you open this folder, you'll see the **nanonauts.jpg** file.

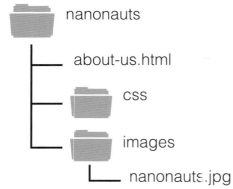

nanonauts

about-us.html

css

images

nanonauts.jpg

 NINJA TIP

If the **nanonauts.jpg** file were missing from the **images** folder then the browser would show a symbol that indicates that. Something like this:

The **src="images/nanonauts.jpg"** is an **attribute**. Attributes always follow the same pattern – the attribute name, followed by an equals sign, followed by an attribute value contained within a pair of straight quote marks. Like this:

attribute name	equals sign	opening straight quote mark	attribute value	closing straight quote mark
src	=	"	images/nanonauts.jpg	"

The **alt** attribute, in the same way, contains text that appears if the picture cannot be shown. This is helpful if the web page is being translated into speech for blind people, for example.

Now that you know how to add a picture, add your own picture into your **about-us.html** page. To do this copy the picture into the **images** folder and then add the code that will display your picture. So, if your picture came from a digital camera and was called **DSC03730.jpg** you might add the following code:

```
<p><img src="images/DSC03730.jpg"
alt="Holly playing the guitar"/></p>
```

TRY IT!

THINGS TO DO NEXT

Try adding some of your own photographs to the page. Add a few selfies!

WORDS TO REMEMBER

Attribute – tags sometimes contain additional information held inside attributes. In the example of the **img** tag below we can see that there are two attributes: **src** and **alt**.

```
<img src="images/DSC03730.jpg" alt="Holly playing the guitar"/>
```

Attributes **always** consist of an attribute name (such as **src** or **alt**) followed by an **=** sign and then by the attribute value contained inside straight quote marks, for example **"images/DSC03730.jpg"**.

The **src** (source) attribute tells the browser where to look for the image. The **alt** (alternative) attribute holds text that will appear if the image cannot be displayed, or if it will be read aloud by screen-reading software.

Element – An element is anything between a start tag and an end tag of the same type. So an **li** element is everything between an **<li>** start tag and an **</li>** end tag.

Empty element – Some elements don't have separate start and end tags: they are called **empty elements**. Examples are:
img – the image element
br – the line-break element

Instead of having a separate end tag they have just a single tag which ends with a forward slash before the closing angle bracket.

```
<img src="images/DSC03730.JPG"
lt="Holly playing a G chord on the
guitar"/> <br/>
```

MORE ONLINE

Adding pictures to pages – http://nano.tips/addpics
Making pictures the right size – http://nano.tips/picsize

‹BUILDING THE SITE›

ADDING NEW WEB PAGES

The Nanonauts now want to make a new page which lists the songs they play. The easiest way to make a new page is to copy an existing page and change it.

Open the **about-us.html** file. Then go to the **File** menu and choose the **Save As** option. Save the file as **our-songs.html.** Notice how the new file appears in the list of files in the **nanonauts** folder. You now have a new web page named **our-songs.html**. But at the moment it's just the same as the **about-us.html** page. You'll need to edit the text so that the page is now a list of songs.
Use the example below for ideas. Add in your own favourite songs!

```
<!DOCTYPE html>
<html>
<head>
<title>Our Songs</title>
<link type="text/css" rel="stylesheet" href="css/my-first-stylesheet.css"/>
</head>
<body>
<h1>Our Songs</h1>
<p>This is a list of the songs we can play:</p>
<ul>
<li>Magical Mystery Bug</li>
<li>Boot It</li>
<li>The Long and Winding Code</li>
<li>Dojo Dancing</li>
<li>Empty Elements</li>
<li>Java Chameleon</li>
</ul>
</body>
</html>
```

When you've finished editing the page, save it and then open the file in your web browser.

NINJA TIP

Every time you save a file in the editor, reload the web page in the web browser to see the effect of your most recent changes. Think **'Save and reload!'**

When the page displays in the browser it looks like this:

Our Songs

This is a list of the songs we can play:

- Magical Mystery Bug
- Boot It
- The Long and Winding Code
- Dojo Dancing
- Empty Elements
- Java Chameleon

The songs are displayed as a **bulleted list** (the little circles to the left of the song names are called bullets). The code for the list is shown below – we'll learn more about lists later.

```
<ul>
<li>Magical Mystery Bug</li>
<li>Boot It</li>
<li>The Long and Winding Code</li>
<li>Dojo Dancing</li>
<li>Empty Elements</li>
<li>Java Chameleon</li>
</ul>
```

Each song in the list is inside an **li** element. An **element** is anything between a **start tag** and an **end tag** of the same type. So an **li** element is everything between an **<li> start tag** and an **</li> end tag**. Notice also that all of the **li** elements are inside a single **ul** element. Can you see the **<ul>** start tag before the first song?

```
<ul>
<li>Magical Mystery Bug</li>
```

And the **</ul>** end tag after the last song?

```
<li>Java Chameleon</li>
</ul>
```

NINJA TIP

Save the page every so often as you're working on it. That way you won't lose your work if your laptop battery runs out suddenly!

THINGS TO DO NEXT

See what happens if you put the **li** elements inside an **ol** instead of a **ul** element.
Figure out:
- ☻ where the **h1** element starts and ends
- ☻ where the **body** element starts and ends
- ☻ where the **html** element starts and ends

The **img** element is an **empty element**: it doesn't have separate start and end tags. See if you can spot another empty element.

Make another page called 'See Us Play' with a file name of **see-us-play.html** which gives the date and time of the Nanonauts' next concert.

17

< BRINGING IT ALL TOGETHER >

MAKING THE HOME PAGE

By now you've made the About Us page, the Our Songs page and the See Us Play page. But to make them into a website you'll need to link them all together so that you can go from one to another. We're going to do that now by making the **home page**.

Open the **about-us.html** file. Then go to the File menu and choose the Save As option. Save the file as **index.html**.

NINJA TIP

Home pages are usually given a file name of **index.html**

Change **index.html** to look like this:

```
<!DOCTYPE html>
<html>
<head>
<title>Home</title>
<link type="text/css" rel="stylesheet" href="css/my-first-stylesheet.css"/>
</head>
<body>
<h1>We are the Nanonauts!</h1>
<p>This is our website. Click on a link to visit a page:</p>
<ul>
<li><a href="about-us.html">About Us</a></li>
<li><a href="our-songs.html">Our Songs</a></li>
<li><a href="see-us-play.html">See Us Play</a></li>
</ul>
</body>
</html>
```

The home page has three **links** on it. They appear inside the **li** elements of a **ul** list. The code to the right is the link to the About Us page.

```
<a href="about-us.html">About Us</a>
```

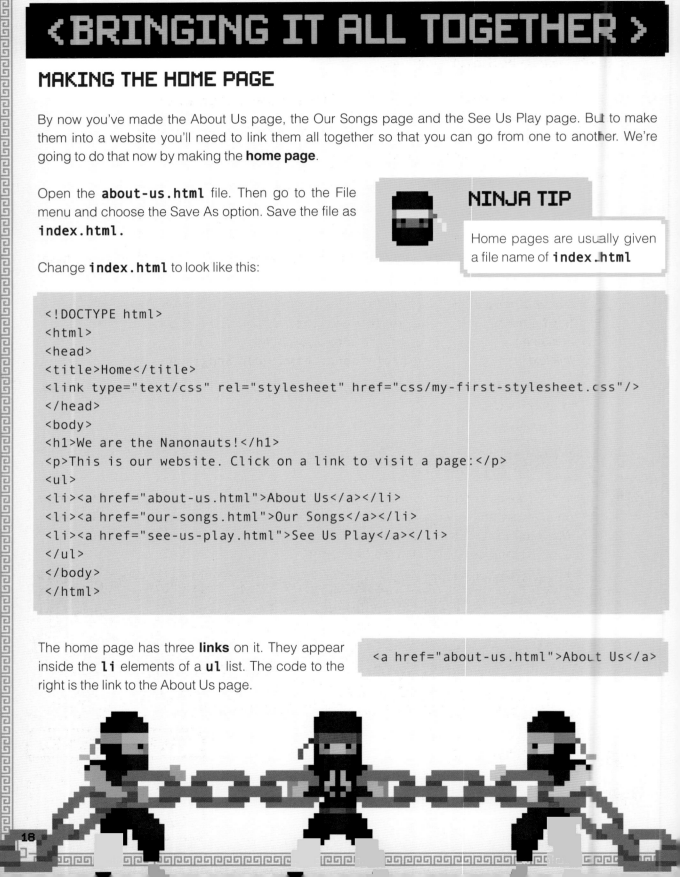

A link has two main parts:

- the bit inside the **href attribute** is the name of the page you want the link to go to. So `href="about-us.html"` would take you to the About Us page.

- the text between the link's opening and closing tags is the text that the reader will click on. Often this text appears underlined on the web page. In our example, the link text will be 'About Us'

If you display the home page in a browser it should look like this:

We are the Nanonauts!

This is our website. Click on a link to visit a page:

- About Us
- Our Songs
- See Us Play

NINJA TIP

Be careful when you're typing links. You have to get them exactly right! They always have the same pattern:

start and end **a** *tags*	`<a href="songs.html">Our Songs</a>`
href *attribute*	`<a href="songs.html">Our Songs</a>`
filename	`<a href="songs.html">Our Songs</a>`
link text	`<a href="songs.html">Our Songs</a>`

Notice how the **href** attribute puts quote marks around the filename and how it comes inside the **a** start tag.

THINGS TO DO NEXT

Make three other pages from the site map. Do it in the same way you made the Our Songs page – save an existing page with a new name and then change the content of the page. When you've made the page, add links to the new pages from the home page.
Some suggestions (your own ideas welcome!):

PAGE NAME	FILE NAME
Choosing Instruments	`choosing-instruments.html`
Playing Songs Together	`playing-songs-together.html`
Tuning Up	`tuning-up.html`
Playing a Concert	`playing-a-concert.html`
Amplification	`amplification.html`
Finding Somewhere to Practice	`somewhere-to-practice.html`

MORE ONLINE

Adding links to pages – http://nano.tips/addlinks

BADGE UNLOCKED

HOME SWEET HOME!

‹HEADINGS, PARAGRAPHS AND LISTS›

The Nanonauts had lots of ideas for what to put on their 'Playing a Concert' page:

"You need a list of the songs you'll be playing, in case you forget what you're supposed to be doing next!" said Holly.

"Don't forget about all the spare bits and pieces you need – like guitar strings or saxophone reeds" said Dervla.

"Set up drums on the stage first," said Sam. "That's my tip. If you leave them till last there might not be enough room for them."

"Make sure you know where you're going" said Daniel. "We were late for Jo's birthday gig because we couldn't find the house."

In fact, they had so many ideas that when they put them all on the page it started to look a little confusing:

Playing a Concert

Playing a concert can be great fun! Or it can be totally scary! Sometimes both at the same time. So we've put together a list of our top tips for great concerts.

Copy out a set-list. A set-list is a list of all your songs in the order you'll play them. Make copies for everyone. Print it big so that you can still read it if it's down by your feet on the floor or if the lighting isn't very good.

Remember your spares. Some instruments have parts that need to be replaced if they wear out or break. For example: guitar strings, saxophone or clarinet reeds and drumsticks. Make a list of the spares you might need and make sure you know where they are in an emergency.

Plan where you'll be on the stage. Before you start to set up your instruments, take a few minutes to decide where you're all going to be. Will the drums be centre stage? Or off to one side? Is there a power-socket for the amplifier if your guitar player stands on the right?

It's much better to think about all this before you start setting up your instruments. It's really annoying if you have to start unplugging things and swapping places once you've begun to set things up! Know where you're going, know when you're on. If you're playing a concert somewhere you've never been before make sure you know where it is. Print out a map or set the sat nav before you set out. There's nothing worse than being lost in an unfamiliar place half-an-hour before you're due to go on-stage. And when you do arrive, the first thing you should do is find out what time you're on. On the night times often change. Ask whoever is running the event when you'll be on. Don't get caught out!

How could they fix it? We've already seen quite a few different HTML elements. For example:

h1 is a heading

ul is a list with bullet points

ol is a numbered list

p is a paragraph

By using these elements and mixing in a few new ones the Nanonauts made their page much easier to read. Like this, in fact:

So how did they do it?

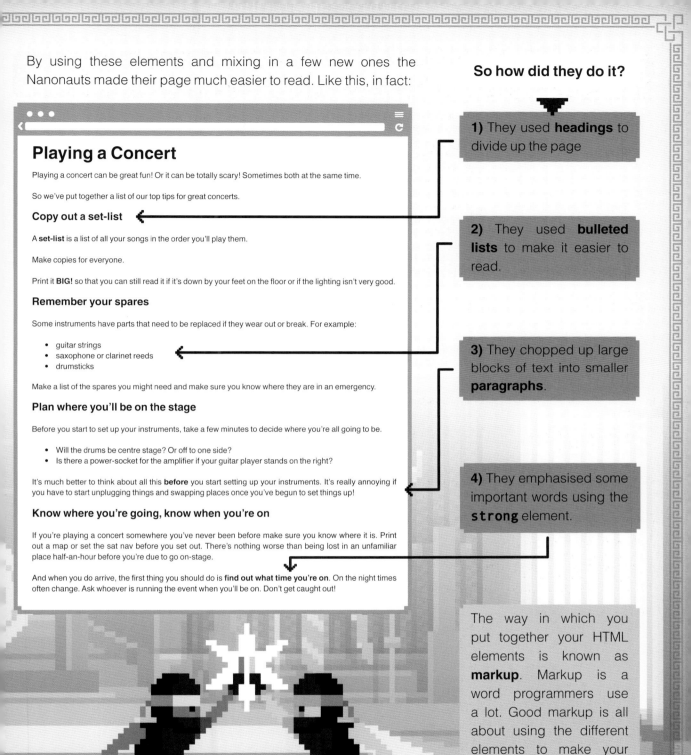

Playing a Concert

Playing a concert can be great fun! Or it can be totally scary! Sometimes both at the same time.

So we've put together a list of our top tips for great concerts.

Copy out a set-list

A **set-list** is a list of all your songs in the order you'll play them.

Make copies for everyone.

Print it **BIG!** so that you can still read it if it's down by your feet on the floor or if the lighting isn't very good.

Remember your spares

Some instruments have parts that need to be replaced if they wear out or break. For example:

- guitar strings
- saxophone or clarinet reeds
- drumsticks

Make a list of the spares you might need and make sure you know where they are in an emergency.

Plan where you'll be on the stage

Before you start to set up your instruments, take a few minutes to decide where you're all going to be.

- Will the drums be centre stage? Or off to one side?
- Is there a power-socket for the amplifier if your guitar player stands on the right?

It's much better to think about all this **before** you start setting up your instruments. It's really annoying if you have to start unplugging things and swapping places once you've begun to set things up!

Know where you're going, know when you're on

If you're playing a concert somewhere you've never been before make sure you know where it is. Print out a map or set the sat nav before you set out. There's nothing worse than being lost in an unfamiliar place half-an-hour before you're due to go on-stage.

And when you do arrive, the first thing you should do is **find out what time you're on**. On the night times often change. Ask whoever is running the event when you'll be on. Don't get caught out!

1) They used **headings** to divide up the page

2) They used **bulleted lists** to make it easier to read.

3) They chopped up large blocks of text into smaller **paragraphs**.

4) They emphasised some important words using the `strong` element.

The way in which you put together your HTML elements is known as **markup**. Markup is a word programmers use a lot. Good markup is all about using the different elements to make your page easy to read.

Here is the HTML for the improved page. Note the new elements like **h1**, **h2** and **strong**.

```
<!DOCTYPE html>
<html>
<head>
<title>Playing a Concert</title>
<link type="text/css" rel="stylesheet" href="css/my-first-stylesheet.css"/>
</head>
<body>
<h1>Playing a Concert</h1>
<p>Playing a concert can be great fun! Or it can be totally scary! Sometimes
both at the same time.</p>
<p>So we've put together a list of our top tips for great concerts.</p>
<h2>Copy out a set-list</h2>
<p>A <strong>set-list</strong> is a list of all your songs in the order you'll
play them.</p>
<p>Make copies for everyone.</p>
<p>Print it <strong>BIG!</strong> so that you can still read it if it's down by
your feet on the floor or if the lighting isn't very good.</p>
<h2>Remember your spares</h2>
<p>Some instruments have parts that need to be replaced if they wear out or
break. For example:</p>
<ul>
<li>guitar strings</li>
<li>saxophone or clarinet reeds</li>
<li>drumsticks</li>
</ul>
<p>Make a list of the spares you might need and make sure you know where they
are in an emergency.</p>
<h2>Plan where you'll be on the stage</h2>
<p>Before you start to set up your instruments, take a few minutes to decide
where you're all going to be.</p>
<ul>
<li>Will the drums be centre stage? Or off to one side?</li>
<li>Is there a power-socket for the amplifier if your guitar player stands on
the right?</li>
</ul>
<p>It's much better to think about all this <strong>before</strong>
you start setting up your instruments. It's really annoying if you have to
start unplugging things and swapping places once you've begun to set
things up!</p>
<h2>Know where you're going, know when you're on</h2>
<p>If you're playing a concert somewhere you've never been before make sure you
```

```
know where it is. Print out a map or set the sat nav before you set out. There's
nothing worse than being lost in an unfamiliar place half-an-hour before you're
due to go on-stage.</p>
<p>And when you do arrive, the first thing you should do is <strong>find out
what time you're on</strong>. On the night times often change. Ask whoever is
running the event when you'll be on. Don't get caught out!</p>
</body>
</html>
```

NINJA TIP

If you look at the Nanonaut's page you can see that they've used the **h2 heading** element
to chop up the text so that you, the reader, can easily find what you're looking for. When
you're marking up a page you should use the **h1 heading** for the main title of the page and
use **h2** elements to provide a heading for each part of the page. You can have as many **h2**
elements as you need.

NINJA TIP

Another thing the Nanonauts have done is divided each of the sections up into paragraphs.
A paragraph is just one or more sentences of text contained inside a **p** element. Think of a
paragraph as being a block of text about a single thought or idea. By splitting up your page
into paragraphs you make it easier for readers to follow what you're saying.

NINJA TIP

The Nanonauts have shown their 'examples of things to remember' as a list with bullet
points. This helps to break up the text, making the page easier to read.

NINJA TIP

Use list markup when you need to make a list of things. There are two kinds of lists: use the **ul** element for **bulleted** ('unordered') lists; use the **ol** element for **numbered** ('ordered') lists. Each list item should be inside its own **li** element.

Bulleted List	Numbered List
`<ul>`	`<ol>`
`<li>rock</li>`	`<li>rock</li>`
`<li>paper</li>`	`<li>paper</li>`
`<li>scissors</li>`	`<li>scissors</li>`
`</ul>`	`</ol>`

Bulleted List	Numbered List
• rock	1. rock
• paper	2. paper
• scissors	3. scissors

You can see that the word 'set-list' and the phrase 'find out what time you're on' are inside **strong elements**. The **strong** elements can be used inside other elements such as **p** and **li**. You use it if you want to make particular words stand out.

NEST YOUR ELEMENTS!

Elements should always be nested. This means that they always slot inside one another, like Russian dolls!

What does 'nested' mean?

When we talk about an element being nested in another element we mean that its opening and closing tags occur somewhere between the other element's opening and closing tags. For example, if we say that a **strong** element containing the word 'Tip' is 'inside' a **p** element we mean that its opening **** and closing **** tags occur somewhere between the opening **<p>** and closing **</p>** tags of the **p** element.

CORRECT

```
<p><strong>Tip:</strong>
If you make a mistake
don't stop playing!</p>
```

INCORRECT

```
<strong><p>Tip:</strong>
If you make a mistake
don't stop playing!</p>
```

MAKING IT LOOK BETTER

So far our web pages look … OK. But they're a bit boring aren't they? They look more like pages in a printed book than webpages. BUT maybe we could change this by:

- changing the background colour of the page
- adding a background picture
- making the text look fancier

We can do all of these things – and more – by changing the stylesheet for the site.

‹LAYING ON THE STYLE!›

If you want to change the appearance of your web pages you don't change the code of the pages themselves. Instead you change the code of the **stylesheet**. We came across the stylesheet earlier in the book. But now we're going to look at it in a lot more detail. Stylesheets are where a lot of the magic happens when you're designing a great-looking website!

In the picture below you can see the exact same HTML web page – the only thing that's changed is the stylesheet.

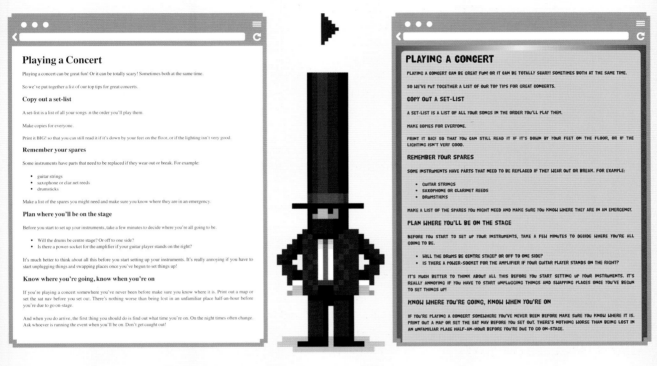

WHAT STYLESHEET IS MY PAGE USING?

If you look at the top part of the code for your web pages you'll see a **link** element below the page title:

```
<!DOCTYPE html>
<html>
<head>
<title>Playing a Concert</title>
<link type="text/css" rel="stylesheet" href="css/my-first-stylesheet.css"/>
</head>
```

By looking at this link you can find the name of the css file which is being used to style the page. The **link** element tells the web browser to look inside the **css** folder for the **my-first-stylesheet.css** file.

WHAT'S IN THE STYLESHEET?

Let's take a look at the stylesheet and see how we can modify it. Open one of your web pages in your browser and open **my-first-stylesheet.css** alongside it in the code editor, so that you can see them both side-by-side. The **my-first-stylesheet.css** file contains just one **rule**.

This rule tells the browser how to format everything inside the **body** element of the HTML file. What this rule is saying is 'display everything in the body element in a sans-serif font'.

```
body {
  font-family: sans-serif;
}
```

So if we change the rule so that the **font-family** is now **serif** – and reload the web page, we see that it suddenly looks different.

```
body {
  font-family: serif;
}
```

Playing a Concert

Playing a concert can be great fun! Or it can be totally scary! Sometimes both at the same time.

So we've put together a list of our top tips for great concerts.

Copy out a set-list

A **set-list** is a list of all your songs in the order you'll play them.

Make copies for everyone.

Print it **BIG!** so that you can still read it if it's down by your feet on the floor, or if the lighting isn't very good.

Remember your spares

Some instruments have parts that need to be replaced if they wear out or break. For example:

- guitar strings
- saxophone or clarinet reeds
- drumsticks

Make a list of the spares you might need and make sure you know where they are in an emergency.

Plan where you'll be on the stage

Before you start to set up your instruments, take a few minutes to decide where you're all going to be.

- Will the drums be centre stage? Or off to one side?
- Is there a power-socket for the amplifier if your guitar player stands on the right?

It's much better to think about all this **before** you start setting up your instruments. It's really annoying if you have to start unplugging things and swapping places once you've begun to set things up!

Know where you're going, know when you're on

If you're playing a concert somewhere you've never been before make sure you know where it is. Print out a map or set the sat nav before you set out. There's nothing worse than being lost in an unfamiliar place half-an-hour before you're due to go on-stage.

And when you do arrive, the first thing you should do is **find out what time you're on**. On the night times often change. Ask whoever is running the event when you'll be on. Don't get caught out!

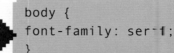

Playing a Concert

Playing a concert can be great fun! Or it can be totally scary! Sometimes both at the same time.

So we've put together a list of our top tips for great concerts.

Copy out a set-list

A **set-list** is a list of all your songs in the order you'll play them.

Make copies for everyone.

Print it **BIG!** so that you can still read it if it's down by your feet on the floor, or if the lighting isn't very good.

Remember your spares

Some instruments have parts that need to be replaced if they wear out or break. For example:

- guitar strings
- saxophone or clarinet reeds
- drumsticks

Make a list of the spares you might need and make sure you know where they are in an emergency.

Plan where you'll be on the stage

Before you start to set up your instruments, take a few minutes to decide where you're all going to be.

- Will the drums be centre stage? Or off to one side?
- Is there a power-socket for the amplifier if your guitar player stands on the right?

It's much better to think about all this **before** you start setting up your instruments. It's really annoying if you have to start unplugging things and swapping places once you've begun to set things up!

Know where you're going, know when you're on

If you're playing a concert somewhere you've never been before make sure you know where it is. Print out a map or set the sat nav before you set out. There's nothing worse than being lost in an unfamiliar place half-an-hour before you're due to go on-stage.

And when you do arrive, the first thing you should do is **find out what time you're on**. On the night times often change. Ask whoever is running the event when you'll be on. Don't get caught out!

MORE ONLINE

If you find opening the stylesheet difficult, see the tutorial at http://nano.tips/stylesheet

Let's change the stylesheet a little more. We'll change the body font back to sans-serif and we'll also make the background a purple colour. So the changed `my-first-stylesheet.css` file will look like this

```css
body {
background-color: Thistle;
font-family: sans-serif;
margin-left: auto;
margin-right: auto;
max-width: 1024px;
min-width: 256px;
padding-top: 8px;
padding-bottom: 24px;
padding-left: 24px;
padding-right: 24px;
}
```

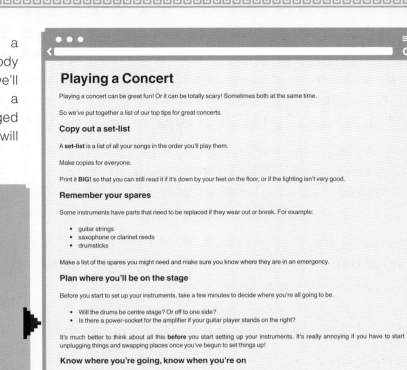

Playing a Concert

Playing a concert can be great fun! Or it can be totally scary! Sometimes both at the same time.

So we've put together a list of our top tips for great concerts.

Copy out a set-list

A **set-list** is a list of all your songs in the order you'll play them.

Make copies for everyone.

Print it **BIG!** so that you can still read it if it's down by your feet on the floor, or if the lighting isn't very good.

Remember your spares

Some instruments have parts that need to be replaced if they wear out or break. For example:

- guitar strings
- saxophone or clarinet reeds
- drumsticks

Make a list of the spares you might need and make sure you know where they are in an emergency.

Plan where you'll be on the stage

Before you start to set up your instruments, take a few minutes to decide where you're all going to be.

- Will the drums be centre stage? Or off to one side?
- Is there a power-socket for the amplifier if your guitar player stands on the right?

It's much better to think about all this **before** you start setting up your instruments. It's really annoying if you have to start unplugging things and swapping places once you've begun to set things up!

Know where you're going, know when you're on

If you're playing a concert somewhere you've never been before make sure you know where it is. Print out a map or set the sat nav before you set out. There's nothing worse than being lost in an unfamiliar place half-an-hour before you're due to go on-stage.

And when you do arrive, the first thing you should do is **find out what time you're on**. On the night times often change. Ask whoever is running the event when you'll be on. Don't get caught out!

Just making these small changes has already made our page look a lot more interesting – But we can do a lot more than this.

LET'S GET

RADICAL!

Change the stylesheet so that it looks like the one below to see just how dramatic an effect a few lines of code can have!

```
body {
background-color: Thistle;
border: 2px solid Gray;
border-radius: 16px;
font-family: sans-serif;
margin-left: auto;
margin-right: auto;
max-width: 1024px;
min-width: 256px;
padding-top: 8px;
padding-bottom: 24px;
padding-left: 24px;
padding-right: 24px;
}
html {
background: radial-
gradient(circle, SkyBlue,
SkyBlue 50%, LightCyan 50%,
SkyBlue);
background-size: 8px 8px;
}
```

Playing a Concert

Playing a concert can be great fun! Or it can be totally scary! Sometimes both at the same time.

So we've put together a list of our top tips for great concerts.

Copy out a set-list

A **set-list** is a list of all your songs in the order you'll play them.

Make copies for everyone.

Print it **BIG!** so that you can still read it if it's down by your feet on the floor, or if the lighting isn't very good.

Remember your spares

Some instruments have parts that need to be replaced if they wear out or break. For example:

- guitar strings
- saxophone or clarinet reeds
- drumsticks

Make a list of the spares you might need and make sure you know where they are in an emergency.

Plan where you'll be on the stage

Before you start to set up your instruments, take a few minutes to decide where you're all going to be.

- Will the drums be centre stage? Or off to one side?
- Is there a power-socket for the amplifier if your guitar player stands on the right?

It's much better to think about all this **before** you start setting up your instruments. It's really annoying if you have to start unplugging things and swapping places once you've begun to set things up!

Know where you're going, know when you're on

If you're playing a concert somewhere you've never been before make sure you know where it is. Print out a map or set the sat nav before you set out. There's nothing worse than being lost in an unfamiliar place half-an-hour before you're due to go on-stage.

And when you do arrive, the first thing you should do is **find out what time you're on**. On the night times often change. Ask whoever is running the event when you'll be on. Don't get caught out!

To understand exactly how rules work, first add **empty rules** like this:

```
body {
}
html {
}
```

Then add in the individual lines (these are called declarations) one at a time. After adding a new declaration save the stylesheet and reload the page in your web browser to see the effect.

So your first step would be to add the **background-color: Thistle;** declaration, like this:

```
body {
background-color: Thistle;
}
html {
}
```

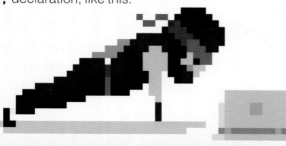

Then add the next declaration,
border: 2px solid Gray;

```
body {
background-color: Thistle;
border: 2px solid Gray;
}
html {
}
```

And so on. This way you get to see what each individual line does. For more information about this technique go to http://nano.tips/declarations

Notice how a rule may contain more than one declaration. Each declaration is ended by a **semicolon** (**;**) and consists of a **property** (such as **color**) followed by a **colon** (**:**) and then a **value** (such as **White**). Declarations are enclosed in curly brackets **{** and **}**. A common mistake is to miss out a semicolon at the end of a declaration or the last curly bracket at the end of a rule.

BADGE UNLOCKED

STYLISH!

WORDS TO REMEMBER

Bullet – A bullet is a small round marker • that appears before the items in a list. In HTML each of the **li** elements inside a **ul** element will normally be displayed with a bullet point in front of it. However, you can use a stylesheet to turn off the display of bullets if you wish.

CSS – Another name for a stylesheet (see below) is a 'CSS file'. CSS stands for 'cascading stylesheet'.

Declaration – A stylesheet contains a set of rules for how your HTML page is displayed. Each rule is made up of one or more declarations such as **background-color: Orange;** or **font-family: sans-serif;**

Font – A particular style of text is called a font. Fonts can come in loads of different styles – you can change the fonts on your web page by using the stylesheet.

Stylesheet – A stylesheet contains the recipe for how your HTML page should look. If you want to change the appearance of a page you do this by changing the stylesheet.
A stylesheet is a list of rules which, together, tell the web browser how to format each element on the page.

COLOURS

We can add colour to our pages in several ways. For example:
- We can set the background colour of an element (we used this to change the background of our Playing a Concert page to purple)
- We can set the colour of the text
- We also can set the colours of borders and links

In fact, just about anything on the page can be coloured.

NINJA TIP

In CSS, we always use American spellings – so we use **color**, not colour, and **Gray** instead of grey. That's just something you'll have to get used to!

Colours can be set in two different ways:
- you can give a name for a colour (such as **Yellow**)
- you can enter a **hexadecimal code** (six characters beginning with a **#** symbol – such as **#B577B5**)

So far we have used the first method, with colours like **Thistle** and **Gray**. Entering a colour name is simple, but what if you don't want the background of your menu to be just '**Blue**', but an exact shade of sky blue? This is where the **hex codes** come in. All the colours you see on your screen are made from a combination of red, green and blue light at different levels of brightness. Hex codes are just a way of setting the red, blue and green values. The first two characters after the # represent the red part, the next two characters represent the green part, the final two characters determine the blue part. Here are some examples:

#000000   #E60000   #0000CC   #FF8C19   #EE82EE   #00E600

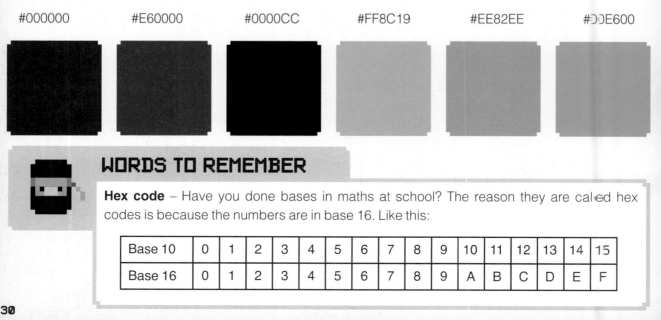

WORDS TO REMEMBER

Hex code – Have you done bases in maths at school? The reason they are called hex codes is because the numbers are in base 16. Like this:

Base 10	0	1	2	3	4	5	6	7	8	9	10	11	12	13	14	15
Base 16	0	1	2	3	4	5	6	7	8	9	A	B	C	D	E	F

This theory is all very well – but how can you actually get the code of a particular colour?

There are two main ways:

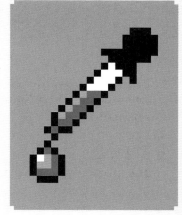

- 👁 If you have an image-editing program such as the The GNU Image Manipulation Program (GIMP), Adobe Photoshop or Corel Paint Shop Pro, you can use the colour picker or colour selector tool. This allows you to hover the cursor over a particular part of an image and get the hex value of the colour. Or you can pop open a window and pick a colour from a colour palette or a colour wheel.
- 👁 If you don't have an image-editing program you can use an online colour picker.

Once you have the hex value of a colour, you can use it in your stylesheet. For example, if C0C0FF is the code for the exact pastel blue colour you want to use as a background colour for your **h1** main heading, simply add the following rule to your stylesheet:

```
h1 {
background-color:#C0C0FF;
}
```

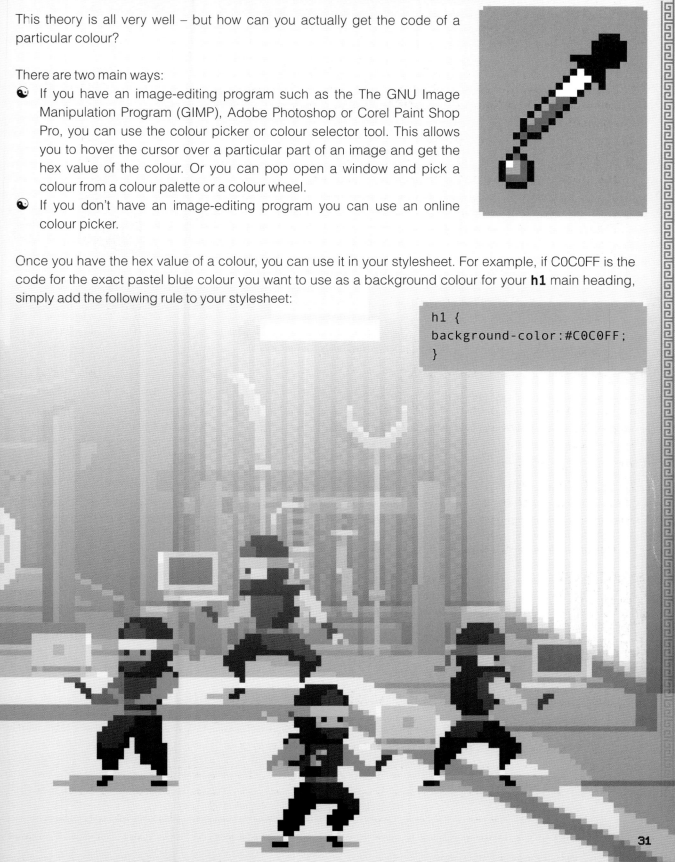

MORE ABOUT MEASUREMENTS

You may have spotted that we use three different types of measurements in our stylesheets: **px**, **em** and **%**. What's the difference and where do we use them?

MEANING

px

Your screen image is made up of tiny dots called **pixels**. The abbreviation for a pixel is **px**. The thinnest line you could see on the screen would be 1px in width. The smallest shape you could see would be a 1px by 1px dot.

em

An **em** is about the width of two letters (we say 'about' because letters have different widths!) We use the em measurement because it is calculated in relation to the font size. So if your font size gets bigger, the width allowed for 50 em will increase. For this reason an em is called a **relative** measurement.

%

When an element has a percentage width, the percentage is measured against the width of the element that contains it (remember that elements are nested inside each other!) So if you set the width of a **img** element which was inside a **p** element to 50% it would be half of the width of the **p** element. Percentage widths are indicated by the **%** symbol.

USE

Use pixels when you want to give an exact width to something. But only if that width should never change, even if the screen gets wider or narrower. For example the width of a border or the amount of padding between the words and the edge of an element.

Use ems when you need to set a maximum or minimum line width for a block of text. Between 40 and 60 em is about the maximum length a line can get before it becomes difficult to follow the words from one line to another.

Using percentage measurements is a good choice when you are creating the overall layout of the web page. We'll use percentage measurements later in this book when we create more complicated page layouts.

‹LINK THE PAGES WITH A MENU›

Although the Nanonauts site now has four pages there isn't an easy way to go from one page to another unless you start from the home page (**index.html**). So we're going to add links to all the pages we've created. This will allow us to go from one page to another no matter where we are in the site. Right now, the only links we have are on the **index.html** home page. To do this we'll open up the **index.html** file, copy the HTML code for the links and then paste it into the other files (**about-us.html**, **our-songs.html**, and so on.) We'll also add a link back to the home page.

TO COPY THE LINKS

```
<body>
<h1>We are the Nanonauts!</h1>
<p>This is our website. Click on a link to visit
a page:</p>
<ul>
<li><a href="about-us.html">About Us</a></li>
<li><a href="our-songs.html">Our Songs</a></li>
<li><a href="see-us-play.html">See Us Play</
a></li>
<li><a href="playing-a-concert.html">Playing a
Concert</a></li>
</ul>
</body>
```

1. Open **index.html** in the code editor and select the HTML code for the links. This code is highlighted. To select the code for the links:

☯ click just before the ul opening tag keep the mouse or touchpad button pressed down and then drag down, highlighting the text as you go.

☯ take your finger off the button when you get to the **ul** closing tag.

☯ when the links are selected, check that you've included ALL of the start and end tags for the ul element.

CORRECT

```
<ul>
<li><a href="about-us.html">About Us</a></li>
<li><a href="our-songs.html">Our Songs</a></li>
<li><a href="see-us-play.html">See Us Play</a></li>
<li><a href="playing-a-concert.html">Playing a Concert</a>
</li>
</ul>
```

INCORRECT

```
<ul>
<li><a href="about-us.html">About Us</a></li>
<li><a href="our-songs.html">Our Songs</a></li>
<li><a href="see-us-play.html">See Us Play</a></li>
<li><a href="playing-a-concert.html">Playing a
Concert</a>
</li>
</ul>
```

2. Copy the links into memory. You can use a keyboard shortcut to do this – such as **Ctrl-C** for Windows and Linux systems or **⌘-C** for Macs. Open one of the web pages you made earlier in the Editor (in the example overleaf, we'll use the Playing a Concert page).

3. Click just before the **h1** opening tag and paste in the links. Add in a link to the Home page, too. After you've pasted the links add a **<nav>** opening tag before the opening **<ul>** tag, and a **</nav>** closing tag after the closing **</ul>** element. This puts our list of links inside a **nav** (short for navigation) element. This makes it clear that this list is special – a list of menu links, rather than a list within a story on a page.

```
<!DOCTYPE html>
<html>
<head>
<title>Playing a Concert</title>
<link type="text/css" rel="stylesheet" href="css/my-first-stylesheet.css"/>
</head>
<body>
<nav>
<ul>
<li><a href="index.html">Home</a></li>
<li><a href="about-us.html">About Us</a></li>
<li><a href="our-songs.html">Our Songs</a></li>
<li><a href="see-us-play.html">See Us Play</a></li>
<li><a href="playing-a-concert.html">Playing a Concert</a></li>
</ul>
</nav>
<h1>Playing a Concert</h1>
```

4. Save the file and then open it in your browser. You can see that the links appear above the **h1** element. They look a bit strange, however. It would be better if they ran across the top in a row like the top menu bar you see on most websites.

THINGS TO DO NEXT

First of all, try to change two things.
- ☯ Add a link to the home page above the About Us link.
- ☯ Then copy the full set of links to all the other pages (except the home page as it already has them).

Put the links in the same place before the **h1** element. So all your pages should have a set of links to the other pages above the **h1** heading.

- Home
- About Us
- Our Songs
- See Us Play
- Playing a Concert

Playing a Concert

Playing a concert can be great fun! Or it can be totally scary! Sometimes both at the same time.

So we've put together a list of our top tips for great concerts.

Copy out a set-list

A **set-list** is a list of all your songs in the order you'll play them.

Make copies for everyone.

Print it **BIG!** so that you can still read it if it's down by your feet on the floor, or if the lighting isn't very good.

Remember your spares

Some instruments have parts that need to be replaced if they wear out or break. For example:

- guitar strings
- saxophone or clarinet reeds
- drumsticks

‹ADDING A MENU›

Having a list of links at the top of the page looks a little weird. But most sites would arrange these links in a menu bar – which would look something like this –

| **Home** | **About Us** | **Our Songs** | **See Us Play** | **Playing a Concert** |

But guess what? Just by using CSS we can turn the list of links into a menu. There's no need to change the HTML code at all. We'll do it by adding the following code to the stylesheet.

This turns the links from a list into a menu bar:

```
nav ul {
list-style-type:none;
background-color:#B577B5;
border: 4px solid #111111;
border-radius: 10px;
font-family:sans-serif;
font-weight:bold;
padding: 16px;
}
nav ul li {
display:inline;
border-right: 2px solid #111111;
padding-right: 8px;
padding-left: 8px;
}
nav ul li:last-child {
border-right:none;
}
nav ul li a {
text-decoration:none;
color:#111111;
}
```

- Home
- About Us
- Our Songs
- See Us Play
- Playing a Concert

| **Home** | About Us | Our Songs | See Us Play | Playing a Concert |

MORE COMPLEX RULES!

In our previous example our rules just had a single element name outside the curly brackets. For example, here are three declarations which set the colour, font family and font size for a single **h1** element.

```
h1 {
color:#111111;
font-family:
sans-serif;
font-size: 32px;
}
```

```
nav ul li {
display: inline;
border-right: 2px
solid #111111;
padding-right:
8px;
}
```

But in the menu example the bits outside the curly brackets get a little more complicated. Instead of just a single element name, we see several element names, separated by spaces. Think of it as an address. This example applies to every **li** that is inside a **ul** that is, in turn, inside a **nav** element.

So the rules would be applied only to list items that were inside **nav** elements – not 'ordinary' lists. To see the effect of each declaration, we'll follow the same method described in the tip on page 28, by adding the empty rules and then adding in the declarations one at a time. If you add in the declarations in the order described below it will help you to understand how the stylesheet works.

1.
```
nav ul {
list-style-type:none;
}
nav ul li {
}
nav ul li:last-child {
}
nav ul li a {
}
```

Removes the bullet points from lists inside **nav** elements. You can change the appearance of the bullet point or remove it completely using the **list-style-type** declaration.

- ☯ **list-style-type: none;** removes the bullet point
- ☯ **list-style-type: square;** changes them to squares.

2.
```
nav ul {
list-style-type: none;
background-color:#B577B5;
}
nav ul li {
}
nav ul li:last-child {
}
nav ul li a {
}
```

Changes the background colour of the list (the **ul** element) to light purple (**#B577B5** is the **hexadecimal** value for this colour).

3.
```
nav ul {
list-style-type: none;
background-color: #B577B5;
border: 4px solid #111111;
}
nav ul li {
}
nav ul li:last-child {
}
nav ul li a {
}
```

Adds a 4-pixel-wide border to the list. The border is solid, rather than dotted or dashed and is a solid black (**#111111** is the hexadecimal value for this colour). Try changing:

- ☯ the pixel width of the border
- ☯ the border style from **solid** to **dotted** or **dashed**
- ☯ the hexadecimal value to one you choose from an online colour-picker (see page 31.)

4.

```
nav ul {
list-style-type: none;
background-color: #B577B5;
border: 4px solid #111111;
border-radius: 10px;
}
nav ul li {
}
nav ul li:last-child {
}
nav ul li a {
}
```

Adds curved corners to the border. Try changing the **border radius** value to see what it does. Try:
• **5px**
• **20px**

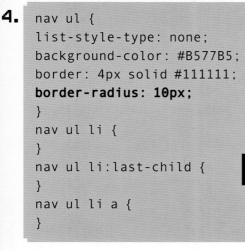

Playing a Concert

5.

```
nav ul {
list-style-type: none;
background-color: #B577B5;
border: 4px solid #111111;
border-radius: 10px;
font-family: sans-serif;
}
nav ul li {
}
nav ul li:last-child {
}
nav ul
```

Makes sure the font is sans-serif. If you don't specify the **font-family**, it will display in the browser's default font. Try changing it to **cursive** or **fantasy** to see what they do.

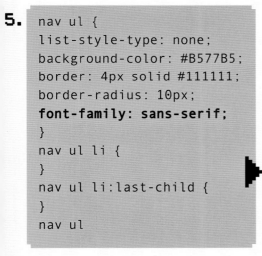

Playing a Concert

6.

```
nav ul {
list-style-type: none;
background-color: #B577B5;
border: 4px solid #111111;
border-radius: 10px;
font-family: sans-serif;
font-weight: bold;
}
nav ul li {
}
nav ul li:last-child {
}
nav ul li a {
}
```

Makes the font heavier and darker looking.

Home
About Us
Our Songs
See Us Play
Playing a Concert

Playing a Concert

Playing a concert can be great fun! Or it can be totally scary! Sometimes both at the same time.

So we've put together a list of our top tips for great concerts.

Copy out a set-list

A **set-list** is a list of all your songs in the order you'll play them.

Make copies for everyone.

7.

```
nav ul {
  list-style-type: none;
  background-color: #B577B5;
  border: 4px solid #111111;
  border-radius: 10px;
  font-family: sans-serif;
  font-weight: bold;
  padding: 16px;
}
nav ul li {
}
nav ul li:last-child {
}
nav ul li a {
}
```

Changes the space surrounding the menu items.
Try changing the padding value.

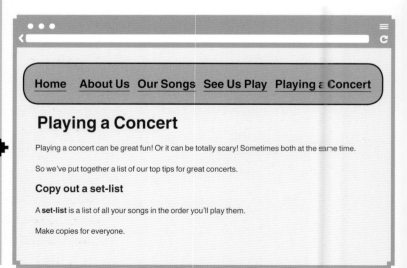

8.

```
nav ul {
  list-style-type: none;
  background-color: #B577B5;
  border: 4px solid #111111;
  border-radius: 10px;
  font-family: sans-serif;
  font-weight: bold;
  padding: 16px;
}
nav ul li {
  display: inline;
}
nav ul li:last-child {
}
nav ul li a {
}
```

Makes the links side-by-side (inline) rather than one above the other. Notice that we have started a new rule here. The previous rule began with **nav ul**. This meant that all the declarations within the rule apply to **ul** elements within **nav** elements. This rule begins with **nav ul li** which means that all declarations within the rule apply to **li** elements – but only if they occur inside **ul** elements within **nav** elements.

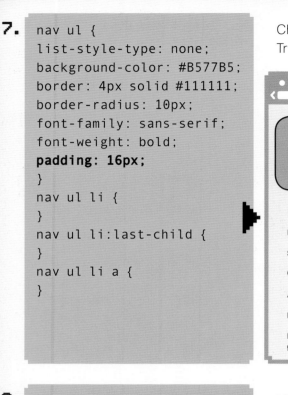

9.

```
nav ul {
list-style-type: none;
background-color: #B577B5;
border: 4px solid #111111;
border-radius: 10px;
font-family: sans-serif;
font-weight: bold;
padding: 16px;
}
nav ul li {
display: inline;
border-right: 2px solid
#111111;
}
nav ul li:last-child {
}
nav ul li a {
}
```

Adds a 2-pixel-wide separator line on the right of each menu entry. You make the line thicker or thinner by changing the number before the **px**. Notice how the declaration combines three separate properties of the border: thickness, line-style and colour.

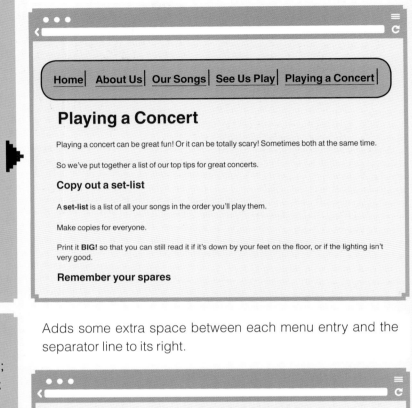

10.

```
nav ul {
list-style-type: none;
background-color: #B577B5;
border: 4px solid #111111;
border-radius: 10px;
font-family: sans-serif;
font-weight: bold;
padding: 16px;
}
nav ul li {
display: inline;
border-right: 2px solid
#111111;
padding-right: 8px;
padding-left: 8px;
}
nav ul li:last-child {
}
nav ul li a {
}
```

Adds some extra space between each menu entry and the separator line to its right.

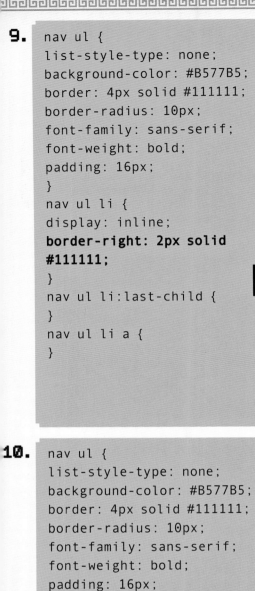

11.

```
nav ul {
list-style-type: none;
background-color: #B577B5;
border: 4px solid #111111;
border-radius: 10px;
font-family: sans-serif;
font-weight: bold;
padding: 16px;
}
nav ul li {
display: inline;
border-right: 2px solid
#111111;
padding-right: 8px;
padding-left: 8px;
}
nav ul li:last-child {
border-right: none;
}
nav ul li a {
}
```

Removes the final separator line. As you can see, we've moved on to a new rule again. This rule begins with **nav ul li:last-child.** The **last-child** condition included in the rule means that it will only apply to the *last* **li** element inside **ul** elements within **nav** elements.

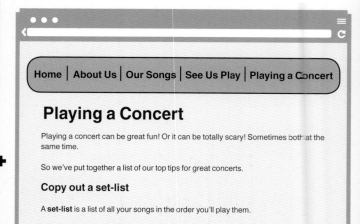

12.

```
nav ul {
list-style-type: none;
background-color: #B577B5;
border: 4px solid #111111;
border-radius: 10px;
font-family: sans-serif;
font-weight: bold;
padding: 16px;
}
nav ul li {
display: inline;
border-right: 2px solid #111111;
padding-right: 8px;
padding-left: 8px;
}
nav ul li:last-child {
border-right: none;
}
nav ul li a {
text-decoration:none;
}
```

Removes the underlining of the menu items. Showing links as underlined is useful in a webpage but doesn't look good in the top menu. We can set the **text-decoration** value to **none** to remove the underlining. The **nav ul li a** part of the rule means it will apply to **a** elements inside **li** elements inside **ul** elements within **nav** elements.

13.

```
nav ul {
list-style-type: none;
background-color: #B577B5;
border: 4px solid #111111;
border-radius: 10px;
font-family: sans-serif;
font-weight: bold;
padding: 16px;
}
nav ul li {
display: inline;
border-right: 2px solid
#111111;
padding-right: 8px;
padding-left: 8px;
}
nav ul li:last-child {
border-right: none;
}
nav ul li a {
text-decoration:none;
color:#111111;
}
```

Ensures the link colour is black. To complete our menu, we change the links to black to blend in with the rest of the menu bar's colour scheme.

Home │ About Us │ Our Songs │ See Us Play │ Playing a Concert

Playing a Concert

Playing a concert can be great fun! Or it can be totally scary! Sometimes both at the same time.

So we've put together a list of our top tips for great concerts.

Copy out a set-list

A **set-list** is a list of all your songs in the order you'll play them.

Make copies for everyone.

Print it **BIG!** so that you can still read it if it's down by your feet on the floor, or if the lighting isn't very good.

Remember your spares

Some instruments have parts that need to be replaced if they wear out or break. For example:

- guitar strings
- saxophone or clarinet reeds
- drumsticks

BADGE UNLOCKED
MENU MASTERY!

‹FORMATTING A PARTICULAR PART OF THE PAGE›

You may remember that when we added the menu we surrounded it with a **nav** element. Like this.

By doing this we make the code easier to read and also make it possible to add rules in the stylesheet that applied only to the menu.

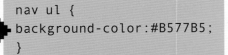

```
<nav>
<ul>



</ul>
</nav>
```

The rule to the right will change only the background colours of **ul** elements inside a **nav** element.

```
nav ul {
background-color:#B577B5;
}
```

This list would have a light purple background colour:

```
<body>
<nav>
<ul>
<li><a href="index.html">Home</a></li>
<li><a href="about-us.html">About Us</a></li>
<li><a href="our-songs.html">Our Songs</a></li>
<li><a href="see-us-play.html">See Us Play</a></li>
<li><a href="playing-a-concert.html">Playing a Concert</a></li>
</ul>
</nav>
```

But this list will NOT have a light purple background colour:

```
<body>
<ul>
<li><a href="index.html">Home</a></li>
<li><a href="about-us.html">About Us</a></li>
<li><a href="our-songs.html">Our Songs</a></li>
<li><a href="see-us-play.html">See Us Play</a></li>
<li><a href="playing-a-concert.html">Playing a
Concert</a></li>
</ul>
```

If you added the rule below, it would change the background colours of both lists.

```
ul {
background-
color:#B577B5;
}
```

Also notice that you can make rules for elements that apply only when they appear inside other elements.

So the rule to the right applies to **li** elements **only** if they are inside a **ul** element which is, in turn, inside a **nav** element. We'll make use of this technique (its proper name is **contextual selection**) later on when we'll be designing some much more complicated pages.

```
nav ul li {
display: inline;
border-right:   2px
solid #111111;
padding-right: 8px;
}
```

<I'M SPECIAL! USING THE class ATTRIBUTE>

Another way to identify elements which have a special meaning and which should be styled in a particular way is to use a **class** attribute.

LET'S SEE HOW THIS WORKS ...

The Nanonauts have decided that they want to include 'top tips' for musicians on some of the pages. They want these tips to stand out from the rest of the page – like this:

TOP TIP: If you hit a wrong note or make a mistake, don't stop playing – just carry on and look as though you meant it!

The first thing they do is, in the HTML page, add a **class** attribute to a **p** element which contains the tip. Like this:

```
<p class="top-tip">If you hit a wrong note or make
a mistake, don't stop playing – just carry on and
look as though you meant it!</p>
```

The Nanonauts then use the stylesheet to format the tips in a special way so that they stand out. Here are the rules they use to format the top tip:

```
p.top-tip {
border:4px solid
#00AFEB;
border-radius:10px;
padding:16px;
background-color:
#C5EBFB;
}
p.top-tip::before {
color:Black;
content:"TOP TIP: ";
font-weight:bold;
}
```

THINGS TO DO NEXT

See if you can add some top tips to your pages.
- ☯ Can you figure out what the **p.top-tip:before** rule does?
  Hint: try changing **content: "Top Tip: ";** to **content: "Mega Tip! ";**
- ☯ Can you make just the words Top Tip: appear in orange?
- ☯ What happens if you change the border from **solid** to **dashed**?

MORE ONLINE

If you want to make a web page look really good, it's important that you can pick out the various parts of the page. The **class** attribute has a hidden secret which allows you to apply more than one formatting rule to an element. Find out about the **class** attribute here: http://nano.tips/class

WORDS TO REMEMBER

Class attribute – we've already seen what an attribute is. Most attributes can only be used with particular elements, but the **class** attribute is special because it can be applied to any HTML element. For example:

```
<p class="top-tip">
<h3 class="author">
<table class="football-league-table">
<li class="selected-menu-item">
```

You use the **class** attribute to identify the meaning of a particular element and you can then apply a special style only to the element with that particular class.

BADGE UNLOCKED

CLASSY!

‹LINKING AND EMBEDDING VIDEOS›

If you were thinking of booking the Nanonauts to play at your party you'd want to see them first, right? Well, thanks to video-sharing sites such as YouTube and Vimeo, it's possible to do just that. And because the Nanonauts have already shared a few of their performances on YouTube it should just be a matter of linking to these videos. So what's the best way of doing this?

LINKING TO YOUTUBE

One method would be to provide a link to the video on YouTube. So if you clicked the link you'd be taken to the YouTube page. To do this

1. Go to the YouTube page which shows the video.
2. Click the Share icon.
3. Click the Share option.
4. Copy the **URL** that appears in the Share box.

➡ Share

> # https://youtu.be/dQw4w9WgXcQ

Create a link to the URL like this:

```
<a href="https://youtu.be/dQw4w9WgXcQ">Visit the Nanonauts on YouTube!</a>
```

This is a bit boring though – and it takes you away from the Nanonauts' site and sends you off to YouTube. Wouldn't it be better to show the videos on a page on the site, so that you could play them without having to leave? Luckily there's a really easy way to do this – it's called **embedding** a video.

EMBEDDING A YOUTUBE VIDEO

To embed a video, once again go to the YouTube page which shows the video and click the Share icon. However, this time:

1. Click the **Embed** option.
2. Copy the code that appears in the Embed box.

```
<iframe width="560" height="315" src="https://www.youtube.com/embed/dQw4w9WgXcQ" frameborder="0" allowfullscreen></iframe>
```

3. Paste this code into the HTML for the page on which you want the video to appear. For example, we could add the video so that it appeared after the list of songs on the Our Songs page.

The code for the whole of the Our Songs page now looks like this (note that we've also added the top menu since the version on page 16).

```html
<!DOCTYPE html>
<html>
<head>
<title>Our Songs</title>
<link type="text/css" rel="stylesheet" href="css/my-first-stylesheet.css"/>
</head>
<body>
<nav>
<ul>
<li><a href="index.html">Home</a></li>
<li><a href="about-us.html">About Us</a></li>
<li><a href="our-songs.html">Our Songs</a></li>
<li><a href="see-us-play.html">See Us Play</a></li>
<li><a href="playing-a-concert.html">Playing a Concert</a></li>
</ul>
</nav>
<h1>Our Songs</h1>
<p>This is a list of the songs we can play:</p>
<ul>
<li>Magical Mystery Bug</li>
<li>Boot It</li>
<li>The Long and Winding Code</li>
<li>Dojo Dancing</li>
<li>Empty Elements</li>
<li>Java Chameleon</li>
</ul>
<p>This is a video of us playing some of the songs!</p>
<iframe width="420" height="315" src="https://www.youtube.com/embed/
dQw4w9WgXcQ" frameborder="0"
allowfullscreen></iframe>
</body>
</html>
```

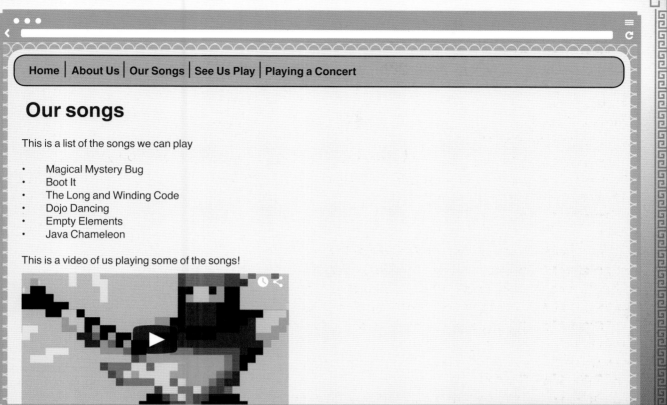

Home | About Us | Our Songs | See Us Play | Playing a Concert

Our songs

This is a list of the songs we can play

- Magical Mystery Bug
- Boot It
- The Long and Winding Code
- Dojo Dancing
- Empty Elements
- Java Chameleon

This is a video of us playing some of the songs!

THINGS TO DO NEXT

Find the embedded video in the code opposite. Can you change the size? Change the **src** attribute by adding **#t=1m30s** to the end:

```
src="https://www.youtube.com/embed/dQw4w9WgXcQ#t=1m30s"
```

What effect does this have?

MORE ONLINE

This page gives you more information about embedding options: http://nano.tips/embedvideo

⟨EMBEDDING A MAP⟩

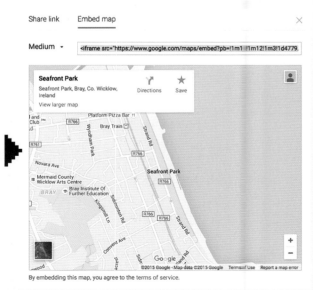

If you can embed a YouTube video you can also embed a Google Map. The way you do it is very similar. The Nanonauts' next concert is at the bandstand in Seafront Park at their home town of Bray, Ireland. Let's see how they add a map to a page showing the location of Seafront Park.

1. PINPOINT THE LOCATION

In the address box on Google Maps, enter the address for Seafront Park

     Search Google Maps   🔍 | ◆

Google Maps will mark the location with a red 'pin' on the map

2. GET THE EMBED CODE

Click the Share button. A dialog box pops up – choose the Embed Map option.

The Embed Map option now allows you to drag and resize the map until you have just the view you want.

When you are happy you have the right view, select the code from the Embed bar and then copy it to the computer's memory (remember the copy shortcuts – **Ctrl-C** for Windows and Linux systems or **⌘-C** for Macs).

3. PASTE THE EMBED CODE INTO THE WEBPAGE

The Nanonauts add the map to the See Us Play page. Here is the code for the main part of their page. The embedded code for the map is pasted after the details of the concert.

```
<h1>See Us Play!</h1>
<h2>Our Next Concert</h2>
<p>Is at the bandstand, Bray Seafront Park on Saturday, 18th June at 4:00pm</p>
<p>Admission is <strong>free!</strong></p>
<iframe src="https://www.google.com/maps/embed?pb=!1m18!1m12!1m3!1d2389.76841
5129388!2d-6.1004805846458385!3d53.20406939306039!2m3!1f0!2f0!3f0!3m2!1i1024!
2i768!4f13.1!3m3!1m2!1s0x4867a8680bea21b5%3A0x6c1f35aeb7249ff7!2sBray+Promena
de%2C+Bray%2C+Co.+Wicklow%2C+Ireland!5e0!3m2!1sen!2suk!4v1450275739107" width
="600" height="450" frameborder="0" style="border:0" allowfullscreen>
</iframe>
```

The Google Map will now appear embedded in the webpage.

ADDING A TABLE

The See Us Play page only shows information about the next Nanonauts concert. But they have quite a few concerts coming up and it would be good if there was a list of these concerts. The list could show:
- ☯ the date of the concert
- ☯ where the concert is taking place
- ☯ what time the Nanonauts are playing
- ☯ how much it will cost to get in

A good way to do this would be to show the information in a table. Something like this:

UPCOMING CONCERTS

Date	Place	Time	Price
Sunday, 12th June	Greystones Theatre	7:30 pm	€5.00
Wednesday, 15th June	Presentation College, Bray	8:00 pm	Free!
Saturday, 10th July	Bray Bandstand	11:00 am	Free!
Sunday, 11th July	Bray Bandstand	2:00 pm	Free!
Sunday, 28th August	Greystones Theatre	7:30 pm	€5.00

THE TABLE IN HTML

To understand how to add the table to the See Us Play web page we need to understand what the different parts of the table are called. This is shown in the diagram below:

table row ➤	table header	table header	table header	table header
table row ➤	table data	table data	table data	table data
table row ➤	table data	table data	table data	table data
table row ➤	table data	table data	table data	table data
table row ➤	table data	table data	table data	table data
table row ➤	table data	table data	table data	table data

From this we can see that, in HTML, the recipe for a table is:

1. Add one or more table row elements
2. Fill each row with table header or table data elements. The HTML elements are named as shown to the right.

table row	tr
table header	th
table data	td

If we use the element names, our diagram looks like this:

tr →	th	th	th	th
tr →	td	td	td	td
tr →	td	td	td	td
tr →	td	td	td	td
tr →	td	td	td	td
tr →	td	td	td	td

From this we can see what the actual HTML markup should look like if the table was empty:

```
<h2>Upcoming Concerts</h2>
<table>
<tr>
<th></th><th></th><th></th><th></th>
</tr>
<tr>
<td></td><td></td><td></td><td></td>
</tr>
<tr>
<td></td><td></td><td></td><td></td>
</tr>
<tr>
<td></td><td></td><td></td><td></td>
</tr>
<tr>
<td></td><td></td><td></td><td></td>
</tr>
<tr>
<td></td><td></td><td></td><td></td>
</tr>
</table>
```

We call this the **table skeleton**, because it's just the bones of the table. We haven't added the actual content yet.

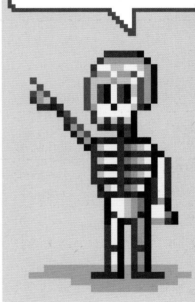

NINJA TIP

If you're creating a table, it's best to begin by working out how many rows and columns your table will have and then creating the skeleton, otherwise tables can get pretty confusing. Make sure when you create the skeleton that all the opening and closing tags are in the correct place. Notice how there are four **th** elements in the first row and then four **td** elements in the following rows. These tags are surrounded by **tr** opening and closing tags.

And finally, we add the content, which will make it look like the code below. Now we've added the table content, we can refresh the See Us Play page to view the result.

```
<h2>Upcoming Concerts</h2>
<table>
<tr><th>Date</th><th>Place</th><th>Time</th><th>Price</th>
</tr>
<tr>
<td>Sunday, 12th June</td><td>Theatre</td><td>7:30 pm</td><td>€5.00</td>
</tr>
<tr>
<td>Wednesday, 15th June</td><td>College</td><td>8:00 pm</td><td>Free!</td>
</tr>
<tr>
<td>Saturday, 10th July</td><td>Bandstand</td><td>11:00 am</td><td>Free!</td>
</tr>
<tr>
<td>Sunday, 11th July</td><td>Bandstand</td><td>2:00 pm</td><td>Free!</td>
</tr>
<tr>
<td>Sunday, 28th August</td><td>Theatre</td><td>7:30 pm</td><td>€5.00</td>
</tr>
</table>
```

It looks a little jumbled up at the moment – but some work with our stylesheet should soon fix that!

Upcoming Concerts

Date	Place	Time	Price
Sunday, 12th June	Theatre	7:30 pm	€5.00
Wednesday, 15th June	College	8:00 pm	Free!
Saturday, 10th July	Bandstand	11:00 am	Free!
Sunday, 11th July	Bandstand	2:00 pm	Free!
Sunday, 28th August	Theatre	7:30 pm	€5.00

A STYLISH TABLE!

To make our jumbled-up table look more attractive we'll return to our CSS stylesheet. Go through the steps below, adding one line at a time to the stylesheet and clicking the refresh button on your web browser after each new line has been added.

1.

```
table {
font-size:70%;
}
th, td {
}
th {
}
td {
}
```

Makes all the text inside the table smaller. The value is entered as a percentage of the font size on the rest of the page.

Date	Place	Time	Price
Sunday, 12th June	Theatre	7:30 pm	€5.00
Wednesday, 15th June	College	8:00 pm	Free!
Saturday, 10th July	Bandstand	11:00 am	Free!
Sunday, 11th July	Bandstand	2:00 pm	Free!
Sunday, 28th August	Theatre	7:30 pm	€5.00

2.

```
table {
font-size:70%;
width: 100%;
}
th, td {
}
th {
}
td {
}
```

Makes the table cover the full width of the body area.

Date	Place	Time	Price
Sunday, 12th June	Theatre	7:30 pm	€5.00
Wednesday, 15th June	College	8:00 pm	Free!
Saturday, 10th July	Bandstand	11:00 am	Free!
Sunday, 11th July	Bandstand	2:00 pm	Free!
Sunday, 28th August	Theatre	7:30 pm	€5.00

3.

```
table {
font-size:70%;
width: 100%;
}
th, td {
border:1px solid
#000000;
}
th {
}
td {
}
```

Adds a 1-pixel-wide, solid, black border to each **th** and **td** element in the table. Notice that each element has its own separate border. This is not the effect we're looking for so we'll fix that next. The first part of the rule is **th, td** which, thanks to the comma between the element names, means 'apply this rule to **th and td** elements'.

Date	Place	Time	Price
Sunday, 12th June	Theatre	7:30 pm	€ 5.00
Wednesday, 15th June	College	8:00 pm	Free!
Saturday, 10th July	Bandstand	11:00 am	Free!
Sunday, 11th July	Bandstand	2:00 pm	Free!
Sunday, 28th August	Theatre	7:30 pm	€ 5.00

53

4.

```
table {
font-size:70%;
border-collapse:
collapse;
width: 100%;
}
th, td {
border:1px solid
#000000;
}
th {
}
td {
}
```

We return to the table rule and set the **border-collapse** property to **collapse**. This merges the borders of the individual cells, creating a nicer visual effect.

Date	Place	Time	Price
Sunday, 12th June	Theatre	7:30 pm	€5.00
Wednesday, 15th June	College	8:00 pm	Free!
Saturday, 10th July	Bandstand	11:00 am	Free!
Sunday, 11th July	Bandstand	2:00 pm	Free!
Sunday, 28th August	Theatre	7:30 pm	5.00

5.

```
table {
font-size:70%;
border-collapse:
collapse;
width: 100%;
}
th, td {
border:1px solid
#000000;
padding:8px;
}
th {
}
td {
}
```

Now we add some padding around the text in the **th** and **td** elements. This makes the contents of the table easier to read.

Date	Place	Time	Price
Sunday, 12th June	Theatre	7:30 pm	€5.00
Wednesday, 15th June	College	8:00 pm	Free!
Saturday, 10th July	Bandstand	11:00 am	Free!
Sunday, 11th July	Bandstand	2:00 pm	Free!
Sunday, 28th August	Theatre	7:30 pm	€5.00

6.

```
table {
font-size:70%;
border-collapse:
collapse;
width: 100%;
}
th, td {
border:1px solid
#000000;
padding:8px;
text-align: left;
}
th {
}
td {
}
```

The header text looks unbalanced centred, so we align it to the left.

Date	Place	Time	Price
Sunday, 12th June	Theatre	7:30 pm	€5.00
Wednesday, 15th June	College	8:00 pm	Free!
Saturday, 10th July	Bandstand	11:00 am	Free!
Sunday, 11th July	Bandstand	2:00 pm	Free!
Sunday, 28th August	Theatre	7:30 pm	5.00

7.

```
table {
font-size:70%;
border-collapse:
collapse;
width: 100%;
}
th, td {
border:1px solid
#000000;
padding:8px;
text-align: left;
}
th {
background-color:
#FCAB68;
}
td {
}
```

We'd like to make the heading row stand out from the rest of the table, so we change its background colour. We use a shade of orange that will complement the background colour of the table. (**#FCAB68** is the hexadecimal value for this shade).

Date	Place	Time	Price
Sunday, 12th June	Theatre	7:30 pm	€5.00
Wednesday, 15th June	College	8:00 pm	Free!
Saturday, 10th July	Bandstand	11:00 am	Free!
Sunday, 11th July	Bandstand	2:00 pm	Free!
Sunday, 28th August	Theatre	7:30 pm	€5.00

8.

```
table {
font-size:70%;
border-collapse:
collapse;
width: 100%;
}
th, td {
border:1px solid
#000000;
padding:8px;
text-align: left;
}
th {
background-color:
#FCAB68;
}
td {
background-color:
#BA99C0;
}
```

And finally we decide to use a dark shade of purple (**#BA99C0**) for the background to the main part of the table.

Date	Place	Time	Price
Sunday, 12th June	Theatre	7:30 pm	€ 5.00
Wednesday, 15th June	College	8:00 pm	Free!
Saturday, 10th July	Bandstand	11:00 am	Free!
Sunday, 11th July	Bandstand	2:00 pm	Free!
Sunday, 28th August	Theatre	7:30 pm	€ 5.00

For a more detailed look at colours and how you can choose them, turn back to page 30.

HELPING YOU GET AROUND

STYLING THE MENU LINKS

The Nanonauts would like to make some changes to the top menu to make it easier for users of the site to find their way from one page to another. There are two things they'd like to do:

- ☯ when you land on, for example, the See Us Play page, the See Us Play menu item should appear in light grey rather than black and you shouldn't be able to click it, because it would take you to the page you're already on!

Home | About Us | Our Songs | See Us Play | Playing a Concert

- ☯ when you roll over the other menu items, the links should change to underlined to show that they are clickable.

Home | About Us | Our Songs | See Us Play | Playing a Concert

To style your links like those above you'll need to edit both the HTML files and the CSS file.

1. In each of your HTML files remove the link from each menu that leads to the same page. For example, in the **about-us.html** page you will remove the **<a href="about-us.html">** link, in the **playing-a-concert.html** page you will remove the **<a href="playing-a-concert.html">** link, and so on.

2. Add a **class** attribute with a value of **selected** to the **li** elements from which you removed the link. The two changes are shown in the before and after tables below.

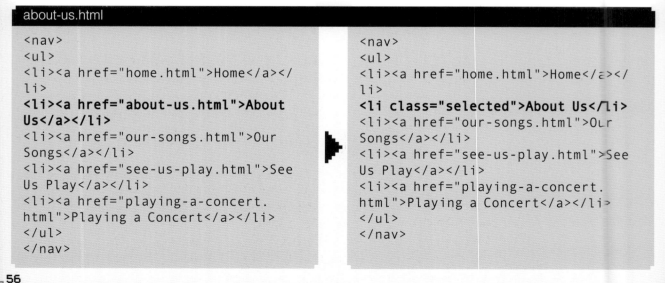

Menu code before editing	Menu code after editing

about-us.html

```
<nav>
<ul>
<li><a href="home.html">Home</a></
li>
<li><a href="about-us.html">About
Us</a></li>
<li><a href="our-songs.html">Our
Songs</a></li>
<li><a href="see-us-play.html">See
Us Play</a></li>
<li><a href="playing-a-concert.
html">Playing a Concert</a></li>
</ul>
</nav>
```

```
<nav>
<ul>
<li><a href="home.html">Home</a></
li>
<li class="selected">About Us</li>
<li><a href="our-songs.html">Our
Songs</a></li>
<li><a href="see-us-play.html">See
Us Play</a></li>
<li><a href="playing-a-concert.
html">Playing a Concert</a></li>
</ul>
</nav>
```

```
<nav>
<ul>
<li><a href="home.html">Home</a></li>
<li><a href="about-us.html">About Us</a></li>
<li><a href="our-songs.html">Our Songs</a></li>
<li><a href="see-us-play.html">See Us Play</a></li>
<li><a href="playing-a-concert.html">Playing a Concert</a></li>
</ul>
</nav>
```

```
<nav>
<ul>
<li><a href="home.html">Home</a></li>
<li><a href="about-us.html">About Us</a></li>
<li class="selected">Our Songs</li>
<li><a href="see-us-play.html">See Us Play</a></li>
<li><a href="playing-a-concert.html">Playing a Concert</a></li>
</ul>
</nav>
```

```
<nav>
<ul>
<li><a href="home.html">Home</a></li>
<li><a href="about-us.html">About Us</a></li>
<li><a href="our-songs.html">Our Songs</a></li>
<li><a href="see-us-play.html">See Us Play</a></li>
<li><a href="playing-a-concert.html">Playing a Concert</a></li>
</ul>
</nav>
```

```
<nav>
<ul>
<li><a href="home.html">Home</a></li>
<li><a href="about-us.html">About Us</a></li>
<li><a href="our-songs.html">Our Songs</a></li>
<li class="selected">See Us Play</li>
<li><a href="playing-a-concert.html">Playing a Concert</a></li>
</ul>
</nav>
```

```
<nav>
<ul>
<li><a href="home.html">Home</a></li>
<li><a href="about-us.html">About Us</a></li>
<li><a href="our-songs.html">Our Songs</a></li>
<li><a href="see-us-play.html">See Us Play</a></li>
<li><a href="playing-a-concert.html">Playing a Concert</a></li>
</ul>
</nav>
```

```
<nav>
<ul>
<li><a href="home.html">Home</a></li>
<li><a href="about-us.html">About Us</a></li>
<li><a href="our-songs.html">Our Songs</a></li>
<li><a href="see-us-play.html">See Us Play</a></li>
<li class="selected">Playing a Concert</li>
</ul>
</nav>
```

3. After you've made the changes, refresh the web page in your browser. Notice that the changed menu entry is no longer clickable. Adding the **class** attribute hasn't done anything on its own. Try refreshing the menu and it'll look the same. But adding the **class** attribute allows you to pick out the link in the **my-first-stylesheet.css** file and change its colour to grey to suggest that it's not clickable. Here's how:

```
my-first-stylesheet.css
```

```
nav ul li a {
text-decoration:none;
}
```

```
nav ul li a {
text-decoration:none;
}
nav li.selected {
color: #606060;
}
```

4. Refresh and you'll see the selected link change to grey. What you've done is added a new rule which applies only to **li** elements with a **class** attribute of **selected**. Notice the syntax in the CSS file – instead of specifying **li** in the rule, you specify **li.selected**

NINJA TIP

nav li.selected means "li elements with a class of selected inside nav elements"

5. Finally, make the links show an underline when you hover over them by adding a new rule to the CSS. This rule defines what will happen when you hover your cursor over an a element.

```
nav li a:hover {
text-decoration:
underline;
}
```

The **:hover** part of the selector is called a **pseudo class**. A pseudo class changes the appearance of an element in certain special situations. The following pseudo classes are available for styling links:

unvisited	Sets how the link should appear before you have visited the link destination.
visited	Sets how the link should appear after you have visited the link destination.
hover	Sets what should happen when you hover the cursor over an element.
active	Sets what should happen when you click on the link before releasing the mouse button.

So a set of rules for link formatting might look like this:

```
a:link {
color: blue;
}
a:visited {
color: purple;
}
a:hover {
text-decoration: underline;
}
a:active {
text-decoration: underline;
background-color: black;
color: white;
}
```

FINISHED!

THINGS TO DO NEXT

- Play around with the various options for formatting links.
- Make some changes to the rules in the example and see what effect it has on your site.

THE CSS BOX MODEL

When you're styling the page using your stylesheet there's a secret to understanding how CSS works – the **CSS box model**. The box model works by imagining that every HTML element is inside a box. This box contains three regions:

- padding
- border
- margin – spacing between this box and the next box

This is shown below.

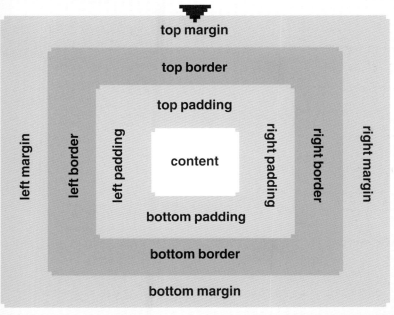

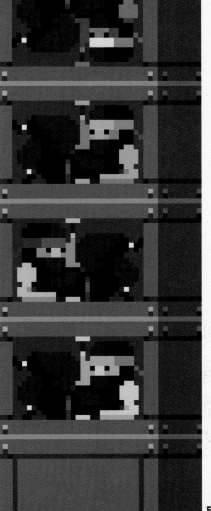

Using the CSS you can change every single part of the box separately. For example you can change the appearance of your headings and paragraphs quite dramatically simply by adjusting the packing and spacing properties.

As well as changing the size of the various parts of the box, you can also change the colours of the different parts of the box. Many of the great visual effects you see on a web page are created in the way.

You can also change the overall size of the box by setting its width or height. Elements that are used to contain individual words or short phrases, such as **em** or **strong** are called **inline elements**. For inline elements, the box fits around the word or phrase. Elements that are used to contain whole paragraphs are known as **block elements**. For block elements, the box normally stretches across the whole width of the page.

These ⟨boxes⟩ have been ⟨*drawn*⟩ around ⟨**inline**⟩ elements.

• This box has been drawn around a block element.

The following tables shows you which common elements are normally block elements and which are normally inline:

We say 'normally' inline or 'normally' block because you can change this in the stylesheet if required. We did this earlier in step 8 of our menu formatting example (see page 38) when we changed the **li** elements inside the menu so that they appeared side-by-side rather than one above the other. We did this by setting the **display** property to **inline** like this:

INLINE	BLOCK
a	h1 to h6
em	p
strong	ul, ol
	li

```
nav ul li {
display: inline;
}
```

A GUITAR TUNER FOR THE SITE

EMBEDDING A SCRATCH PROJECT

After realising how easy it was to embed videos and maps, Holly wondered if she could embed a guitar tuner into the site. But where would she get one from? Then she remembered that her sister had been learning to make games at CoderDojo using the Scratch programming language. She went to the Scratch site and searched for "guitar tuner". There were loads.

She found one she liked but couldn't see any embed option! Fortunately her sister came to the rescue – Holly had to log in to the Scratch site before the Embed button appeared in the information bar at the bottom of the game. The guitar tuner she liked best had the following embed code:

```
<iframe allowtransparency="true"
width="485" height="402" src="//
scratch.mit.edu/projects/
embed/16403918/? autostart=false"
frameborder="0" allowfullscreen></
iframe>
```

Note that the tuner will only show up if your web page is online. For more information on how you get a page online, see page 90.

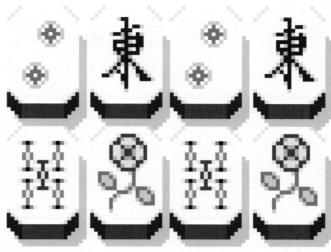

Guitar Tuner

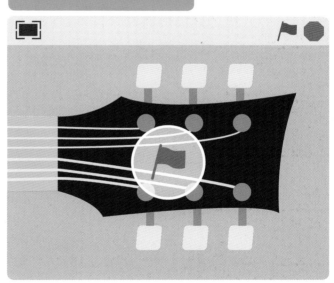

WORDS TO REMEMBER

iframe — you may have noticed that both the YouTube video and the Google map also use the **iframe** element. An iframe allows you to embed content from another site inside your webpage. You specify where to find the content by entering a URL inside the iframe's **src** attribute.

JAVASCRIPT

When you're developing your website, sooner or later you'll encounter **JavaScript**. JavaScript is a programming language which lets you add all kinds of special effects and features to your pages. Things like games, charts and animations. We don't have enough space to show all the things that JavaScript can do in this book, but here is an example to give you an idea of the sort of things you can do. We'll use a simple function that swaps one image for another.

The JavaScript behind the image swapper is embedded inside a page. It's called embedded because the actual JavaScript is in the body of the page inside the **script** element. (You can also put the JavaScript into a separate file if you like. See http://nano.tips/javascript for more information about this and about JavaScript in general.)

```
<!DOCTYPE HTML>
<html>
<head>
<link type="text/css" rel="stylesheet" href="css/full-style.css"/>
</head>
<body>
<p>
<img id="display-image" onclick="swapImage()" src="images/01.png" width="180"
height="180"/>
</p>
<p>Click the image to change it!</p>
<script>
function swapImage() {
var imageDisplayed = document.getElementById('display-image');
if (imageDisplayed.src.match("images/01.png")) {
imageDisplayed.src = "images/02.png";
}
else {
imageDisplayed.src = "images/01.png";
}
}
</script>
</body>
</html>
```

If we look at the code above we can see that the **img** element has an attribute named **onclick** with a value of **swapImage()**.

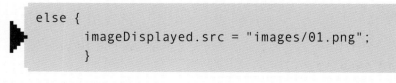

Click the image to change it!   Click the image to change it!

The purpose of the **onclick** attribute is to contain the name of a **function** which will be called when the image is clicked. Function is the name we give to some code which performs a useful task. In this case the **swapImage()** function is contained inside the **script** element. The function begins a series of processes that happen like this:

1. When the image is clicked the **swapImage()** function runs.

▼

```
<img id="display-image" onclick="swapImage()" src="images/01.png" width="180"
height="180"/>
```

2. This makes the image (identified by its **id** of **display-image**) available to the script as a **variable** (**var**) with a name of **imageDisplayed**. (The **id** attribute allows you to give a unique identifying name to an element.)

▼

```
var imageDisplayed = document.getElementById('display-image');
```

3. If the source (**src**) of the **imageDisplayed** variable is currently set to **images/01.png**, then the function changes it to **images/02.png**.

```
if (imageDisplayed.src.match("images/01.png")) {
        imageDisplayed.src = "images/02.png";
}
```

4. However, if the source (**src**) of the **imageDisplayed** variable is currently set to **images/02.png**, then it will change it to **images/01.png**.

```
else {
        imageDisplayed.src = "images/01.png";
        }
```

63

ORGANISING YOUR PAGES

So far we've looked at HTML elements which are used to mark up our text – to organise it into headings, paragraphs, lists and tables. But many web pages have lots of different topics on a single page. Let's imagine that the Nanonauts want to make their About Us page more interesting.

They've decided that they want to have:
- ❂ a short feature about each Nanonaut
- ❂ an advert for their new CD
- ❂ an advert for a new Nanonauts T-shirt
- ❂ details of their next concert

They imagine the page layout might look something like this:

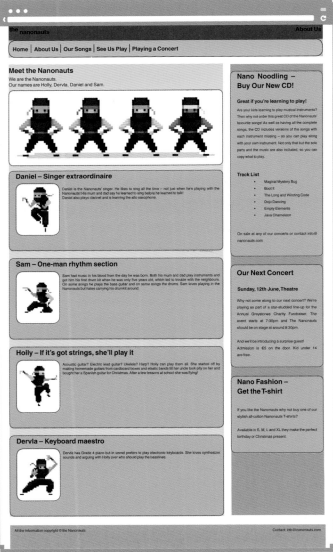

To make it easier for the Nanonauts to organise their page, they can use HTML's **structural elements**. Structural elements allow you to divide up your page so that it's easy to see where one topic begins and another ends. Some of the most commonly used of these structural elements are **header**, **nav**, **article**, **section**, **aside** and **footer**.

Using these elements makes it easier to organise your code and also helps to give you more control over how the page appears.

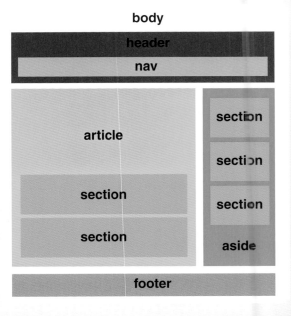

You can also use a technique called **responsive design** to automatically rearrange the content of these structural elements so that the page looks great whether you're looking at it on a mobile phone, a tablet device, a laptop or a PC with a large screen. For example, if you're looking at the page on the small screen of a mobile phone the adverts might appear after you've scrolled down through the main story. But on the wide screen of a desktop PC the adverts could appear side-by-side with the main content.

MOBILE   TABLET

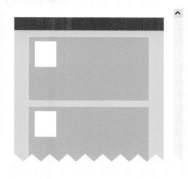

DESKTOP

Let's look at each of these elements in turn.

THE HEADER ELEMENT

The **header** element is often used to contain the web page's logo and title. As the name suggests you usually find it at the top of the page! Sometimes the **header** element also contains the **nav** element.

the nanonauts   About Us

Home | About Us | Our Songs | See Us Play | Playing a Concert

THE NAV ELEMENT

In the case of the Nanonaut's page they use the **nav** element to contain the web page's main navigation. Notice also that the **nav** element is inside the **header** element.

Home | About Us | Our Songs | See Us Play | Playing a Concert

THE ARTICLE ELEMENT

The **article** element is used to contain a single item of content, a section that makes sense on its own without the rest of the page in context. Articles can appear inside articles, a little like Russian dolls!

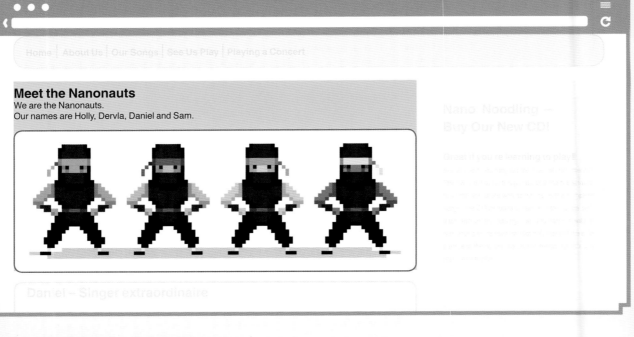

Meet the Nanonauts
We are the Nanonauts.
Our names are Holly, Dervla, Daniel and Sam.

THE SECTION ELEMENT

The **section** element is used to divide a large article into smaller chunks. Each chunk should have a subheading and form a major part of the article. Within the 'Meet the Nanonauts' article, each individual Nanonaut biography can be placed within a section. You can also divide the aside element (see the next page) into sections using the section element.

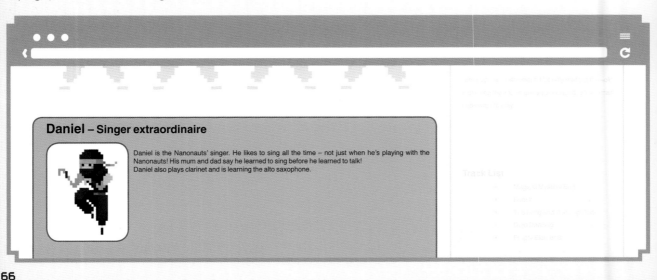

Daniel – **Singer extraordinaire**

Daniel is the Nanonauts' singer. He likes to sing all the time – not just when he's playing with the Nanonauts! His mum and dad say he learned to sing before he learned to talk! Daniel also plays clarinet and is learning the alto saxophone.

THE ASIDE ELEMENT

The **aside** element is used to contain content which isn't really part of the main subject of the page. For example, you often see adverts on a page, or information about up-and-coming events. This sort of content can be placed inside an **aside** element. In the case of the About us page, the adverts for the CD and T-shirt, and information about the next concert can all be placed within the **aside** element.

THE FOOTER ELEMENT

The **footer** element is used to contain content which appears at the bottom of the page. The footer may be the same for every page on the site. Quite often the footer will contain a copyright notice and may contain contact information such as an email address or telephone number.

All the information copyright © the Nanonauts   Contact: info@nanonauts.com

STRUCTURAL ELEMENTS IN USE

THE EXPANDED ABOUT US PAGE

Now the Nanonauts have the basic plan of their site they want to make the individual pages more interesting. They are going to start by adding the extra information described in the last section to the About Us page.

From this –   To this –

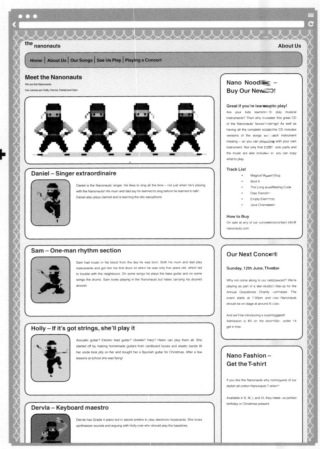

This is the list of things they want to do –

1. Add a header to the page containing the name of the band and the title of the page

2. Add a section called Meet the Nanonauts which contains a short feature about each band member – with their photograph and a few personal details

3. Include adverts for their CD and T-shirt

4. Show details of their next concert

5. Add a footer to the page containing a copyright statement and a contact email address

The code for the page is shown on the next few pages, with the structural elements within the **body** element bracketed in different colours (see the key at the top of page 69 for reference). We also used **indentation** to show the structure more clearly – more on this in a moment. Notice how the **body** element contains the **nav** element followed by a single **article** ('About Us') . The 'Meet the Nanonauts article is split into four **sections** ('Daniel – Singer extraordinaire', 'Sam – One-man rhythm section', 'Holly – If it's got strings, she'll play it' and 'Dervla – Keyboard maestro').

Notice that we haven't given the images a width. Instead we've given each image a **class** – **small**, **medium** or **large** – and we will use the stylesheet to set the image width.

```
<!DOCTYPE html>
<html>
   <head>
      <title>About Us</title>
      <link type="text/css" rel="stylesheet" href="css/my-first-stylesheet.css"/>
   </head>
   <body>
      <header>
         <p>
            <sup>the</sup>nanonauts</p>
         <h1>About Us</h1>
         <nav>
            <ul>
               <li>
                  <a href="home.html">Home</a>
               </li>
               <li class="selected">About Us</li>
               <li>
                  <a href="our-songs.html">Our Songs</a>
               </li>
               <li>
                  <a href="see-us-play.html">See Us Play</a>
               </li>
               <li>
                  <a href="playing-a-concert.html">Playing a Concert</a>
               </li>
            </ul>
         </nav>
      </header>
      <article>
         <h1>Meet the Nanonauts</h1>
         <p>We are the Nanonauts.</p>
         <p>Our names are Holly, Dervla, Daniel and Sam.</p>
         <p>
            <img class="large" src="images/nanonauts-ninjas.png" alt="Picture
of The Nanonauts"/>
         </p>
         <section>
            <h2>Daniel - Singer extraordinaire</h2>
            <p>
               <img class="small" src="images/daniel.png" alt="Picture of
               Daniel"/>
            </p>
            <p>Daniel is the Nanonauts' singer. He likes to sing all the time
- not just when he's playing with the Nanonauts! His mum and dad say he
```

```
learned to sing before he learned to talk!</p>
        <p>Daniel also plays clarinet and is learning the alto saxophone.</p>
    </section>
    <section>
        <h2>Sam - One-man rhythm section</h2>
        <p>
            <img class="small" src="images/sam.png" alt="Picture of Sam"/>
        </p>
        <p>Sam had music in his blood from the day he was born. Both his
mum and dad play instruments and got him his first drum kit when he was only
five years old, which led to trouble with the neighbours. On some songs he
plays the bass guitar and on some songs the drums. Sam loves playing in the
Nanonauts but hates carrying his drumkit around.</p>
    </section>
    <section>
        <h2>Holly - If it's got strings, she'll play it</h2>
        <p>
            <img class="small" src="images/holly.png" alt="Picture of Holly"/>
        </p>
        <p>Acoustic guitar? Electric lead guitar? Ukelele? Harp? Helen
can play them all. She started off by making homemade guitars from cardboard
boxes and elastic bands till her uncle took pity on her and bought her a
Spanish guitar for Christmas. After a few lessons at school she was flying!
</p>
    </section>
    <section>
        <h2>Dervla - Keyboard maestro</h2>
        <p>
            <img class="small" src="images/dervla.png" alt="Picture of
Dervla"/>
        </p>
        <p>Dervla has Grade 4 piano but in secret prefers to play electronic
keyboards. She loves synthesizer sounds and arguing with Holly over who
should play the basslines.</p>
    </section>
    </article>
    <aside>
    <section>
        <h2>Nano Noodling - Buy Our New CD!</h2>
        <h3>Great if you're learning to play!</h3>
        <p>Are your kids learning to play musical instruments? Then
why not order this great CD of the Nanonauts' favourite songs! As
well as having all the complete songs, the CD includes versions of
the songs with each instrument missing - so you can play along with
your own instrument. Not only that, but the solo parts and the music
are also included so you can copy what to play.</p>
        <h3>Track List</h3>
```

```
        <ul>
            <li>Magical Mystery Bug</li>
            <li>Boot It</li>
            <li>The Long and Winding Code</li>
            <li>Dojo Dancing</li>
            <li>Empty Elements</li>
            <li>Java Chameleon</li>
        </ul>
        <h3>How to Buy</h3>
            <p>On sale at any of our concerts or contact <a href="mailto:info@
nanonauts.com">info@nanonauts.com</a>
            </p>
    </section>
    <section>
        <h2>Our Next Concert</h2>
        <h3>Sunday, 12th June, Theatre</h3>
         <p>Why not come along to our next concert? We're playing as part of a
star-studded line-up for the Annual Greystones Charity Fundraiser. The event
starts at 7:30pm and The Nanonauts should be on stage at around 8:30pm.</p>
        <p>And we'll be introducing a surprise guest!</p>
        <p>Admission is €5 on the door. Kids under 14 get in free.</p>
    </section>
    <section>
        <h2>Nano Fashion – Get the T-shirt</h2>
         <p>If you like the Nanonauts why not buy one of our stylish all-cotton
Nanonauts T-shirts?</p>
            <p>Available in S, M, L and XL they make the perfect birthday or
Christmas present.</p>
        <p>
                <img class="medium" src="images/t-shirt.png" alt="Picture of
T-shirt"/>
        </p>
         <p>On sale at any of our concerts or contact <a href="mailto:info@
nanonauts.com">info@nanonauts.com</a>
        </p>
    </section>
  </aside>
  <footer>
      <p class="copyright">All information copyright © the Nanonauts</p>
        <p class="contact">Contact: <a href="mailto:info@nanonauts.com">info@
nanonauts.com</a>
        </p>
  </footer>
  </body>
</html>
```

| body | header | nav | article | section | aside | footer |

STRUCTURE AND INDENTATION

Every HTML page has its own particular combination of elements. Some pages might have lots of headings and paragraphs. Others might have lots of images or tables. The way the elements are arranged is called the page's structure. It's common to show this structure by pushing in the elements from the left margin. An element inside another element is pushed over further than the element it is inside; this is known as indenting. Most HTML editors will show you an indented view of your code. Two simple pages are shown below in indented and non-indented views. Note: indentation does **not** affect how the page appears in the browser, but it makes it easier to understand the structure of your page!

NON-INDENTED

```
<body>
<h1>About Us</h1>
<p>We are the Nanonauts.</p>
<p>Our    names    are    Holly,
Dervla, Daniel and Sam.</p>
</body>
```

```
<body>
<h1>Our Songs</h1>
<p>This  is  a  list  of  the
songs we can play:</p>
<ul>
<li>Magical Mystery Bug</li>
<li>Boot It</li>
<li>The    Long    and    Winding
Code</li>
<li>Dojo Dancing</li>
<li>Empty Elements</li>
<li>Java Chameleon</li>
</ul>
</body>
```

INDENTED

```
<body>
    <h1>About Us</h1>
    <p>We are the Nanonauts.</p>
    <p>Our names are Holly,
    Dervla, Daniel and Sam.</p>
</body>
```

```
<body>
    <h1>Our Songs</h1>
    <p>This is a list of the songs we can
    play:</p>
    <ul>
        <li>Magical Mystery Bug</li>
        <li>Boot It</li>
        <li>The Long and Winding Code<li>
        <li>Dojo Dancing</li>
        <li>Empty Elements</li>
        <li>Java Chameleon</li>
    </ul>
</body>
```

Notice how the various tags are nested inside each other.

We could represent the same information by showing the elements as boxes. If an element is nested inside another element then the boxes are also nested, one inside the other. We can make the structure even clearer by giving each element a different colour. We end up with the diagram shown opposite:

BADGE UNLOCKED

SUPER ORGANISED!

```
<html>

    <body>

        <header>

                <nav>

                </nav>

        </header>

        <article>

                <section>
                </section>

                <section>
                </section>

                <section>
                </section>

                <section>
                </section>

        </article>

        <aside>

                <section>
                </section>

                <section>
                </section>

                <section>
                </section>

        </aside>

        <footer>

        .</footer>

    </body>

</html>
```

We'll make use of this structure in the next chapter. We'll show how you can use CSS to turn these imaginary blocks into real, visible blocks on the About Us page and then style the blocks so that the page looks great!

GETTING RESPONSIVE

Responsive websites are sites that work on all types of devices – desktop computers, laptops, tablets, mobile phones. Responsive websites do this by changing the size and position of the elements on a web page to suit the amount of screen that is available. The diagram below shows how the Nanonaut's About Us page might change its layout depending on the device it is being viewed on.

MOBILE   **TABLET**

DESKTOP

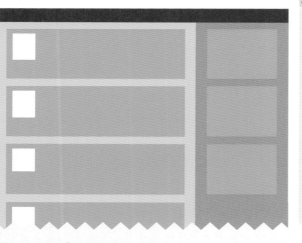

From these examples we can see that:
- mobile or tablet displays can simply stack the elements, one on top of the other.
- desktop machines allow for extra width: the **aside** element (containing the adverts) can move into a right-hand column.

To figure out how best to design a page we can use a **mobile-first** approach. Mobile-first is a popular way to design website pages: first create a design that works well on the smallest mobile device, such as a phone, and then add extra features which make use of the extra screen space available on larger devices.

We're going to use a mobile-first approach to style the About Us page we created previously. To show how this works we're going to go through the following steps:

1. Add coloured backgrounds to the structural elements so that we can easily see how they are being affected by changes in the CSS

2. Style the structural elements so that they look good and are easy to read on mobile phones and larger devices.

3. Add some extra features which will make use of the extra screen space available on larger devices.

Our starting point is the following stylesheet. You can type it in or you can download it from http://nano. tips/stylesheetexample. You can also download the full code of the About Us page if you don't want to type it all in. This stylesheet simply highlights the structural elements by giving each a distinctive background colour. This will make it easy for us to see the effect of applying new CSS rules.

```css
/* technical stuff - set sizing to border
box method */

html {
box-sizing: border-box;
}

*, *:before, *:after {
box-sizing: inherit;
}

/* style the various structural elements */
html {
background-color: Gray;
}

body {
background-color: White;
}

header {
background-color: #F45556;
}

nav {
background-color: #FFCAB68;
}

article {
background-color: #FFD239;
}

section {
background-color: #88BB75;
}

aside {
background-color: #1EADDF;
}

footer {
background-color: #BA99C0;
}
```

NINJA TIP

Use **comments** in your code to let people know what each bit does. (It's also handy if you need to remind yourself!)

Comments start with **/*** and end with ***/** in CSS.

When you add this basic stylesheet skeleton you'll see the various structural elements highlighted in colour (the same colours in the diagram on page 73).

In the rest of this chapter, we will apply the rules one-by-one, like before, so that you can see the effect of each change. We'll start off with the simple stylesheet which displays the elements one on top of the other. We'll finish with a stylesheet which changes where the elements are displayed depending on the width of your browser window.

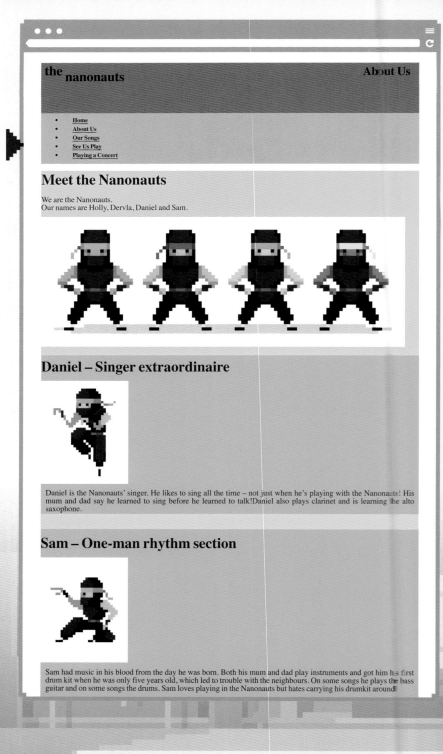

From this:

To this:

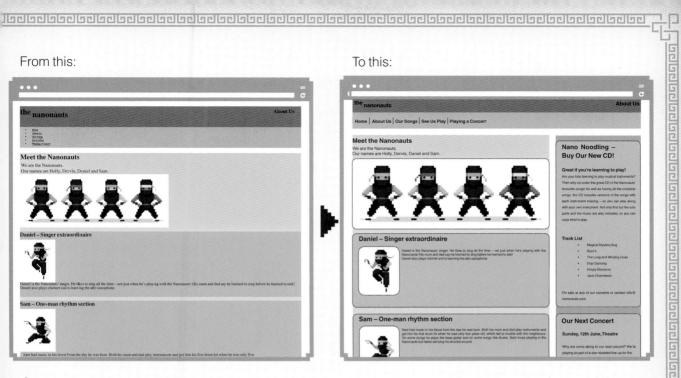

1. We begin by setting the basic dimensions and appearance of the page's **body** element.

☯ we restrict the width to **1024px.**

☯ we set a minimum width of **256px**. If the window gets smaller than this a horizontal scroll bar will appear at the foot of the page.

☯ we set the **margin-left** and **margin-right** properties to **auto**. This makes our body panel stay in the centre of the browser window.

☯ we also set the font style and the text colour.

```
body {
background-color:White;
color:#111111;
font-family:sans-serif;
margin-left: auto;
margin-right: auto;
max-width: 1024px;
min-width: 256px;
}
```

2. Next we set sizes for small, medium and large images. Remember that we used the class attribute to distinguish which images should be small, medium and large. For example `<img class="small"src="images/dervla.png" alt="Dervla"/>`.

```
img.small {
height: 200px;
}
img.medium {
max-width: 360px;
width: 50%;
}
img.large {
width: 100%;
}
```

3. To make better use of the space inside the biography section we can let the small images **float** to the left – so that the text runs around them.

```
img.small {
float: left;
height: 200px;
}
```

NINJA TIP

You can **float** images to the **left** or **right** of text.

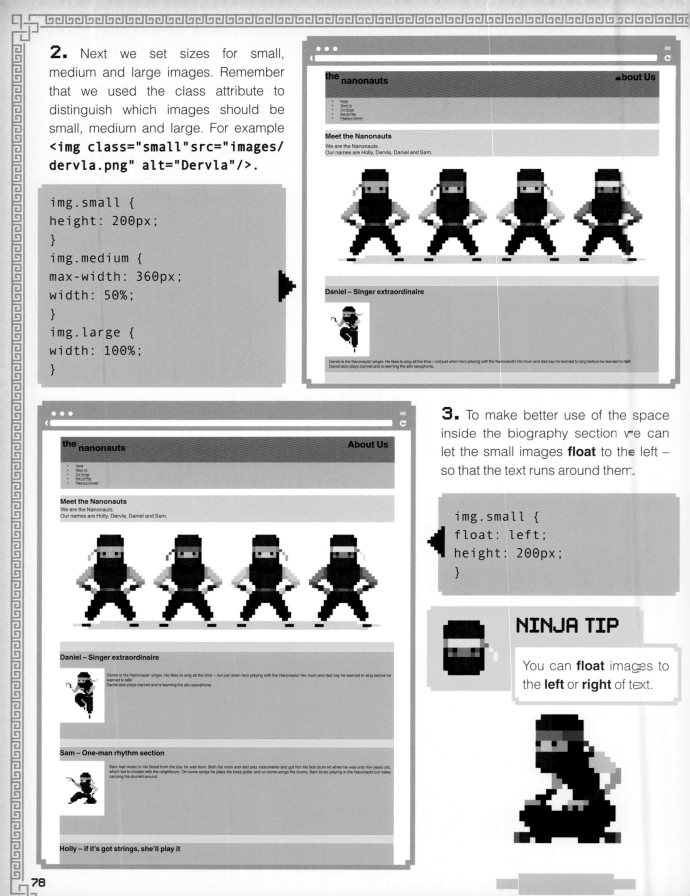

4. Everything is looking a little squashed up against the side of the boxes. It would be nice if there were a little spacing around the edges. To achieve this we add a margin and some left and right padding to the body and section elements, and small images. Add these rules in one line at a time and see the effects.

```
img.small {
float: left;
height: 200px;
margin-bottom: 24px;
margin-right: 24px;
}
```

```
section {
background-color:
#88BB75;
margin-bottom: 24px;
min-height: 320px;
padding-left: 24px;
padding-right: 24px;
}
```

```
body {
background-color:White;
color: #111111;
font-family:sans-serif;
margin-left: auto;
margin-right: auto;
max-width: 1024px;
min-width: 256px;
padding-left: 24px;
padding-right: 24px;
}
```

5. We styled our menu earlier. We can simply drop those styles into our current stylesheet to get ourselves a nice looking menu. Add these rules in one line at a time and see the effects.

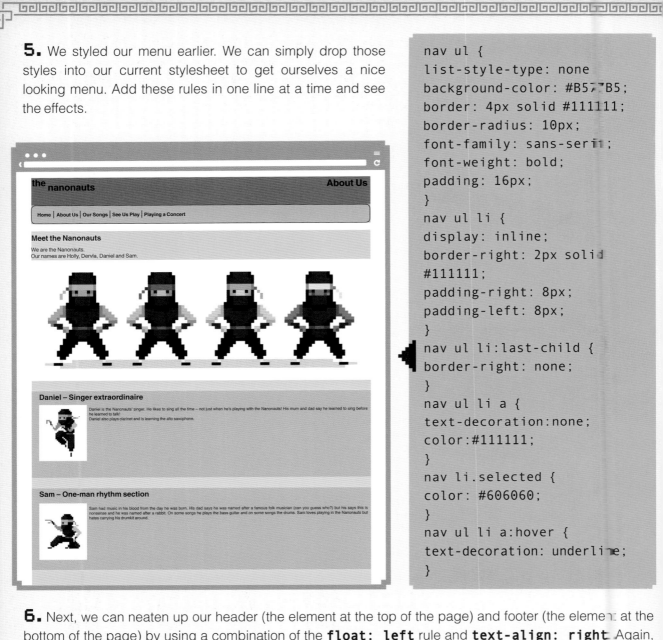

```
nav ul {
list-style-type: none
background-color: #B57FB5;
border: 4px solid #111111;
border-radius: 10px;
font-family: sans-serif;
font-weight: bold;
padding: 16px;
}
nav ul li {
display: inline;
border-right: 2px solid
#111111;
padding-right: 8px;
padding-left: 8px;
}
nav ul li:last-child {
border-right: none;
}
nav ul li a {
text-decoration:none;
color:#111111;
}
nav li.selected {
color: #606060;
}
nav ul li a:hover {
text-decoration: underline;
}
```

6. Next, we can neaten up our header (the element at the top of the page) and footer (the element at the bottom of the page) by using a combination of the **float: left** rule and **text-align: right**. Again, add these rules in one at a time to see the effect they have and how they work together. Notice that we are using contextual selectors to identify all the elements:

header p	means 'any **p** element inside the **header** element'
header h1	means 'any **h1** element inside the **header** element'
footer p.copyright	means 'any **p** element with a class of **copyright** inside the **footer** element
footer p.contact	means 'any **p** element with a class of **contact** inside the **footer** element'

```
header p {
float: left;
font-size: 16px;
font-weight: bold;
margin-top: 0px;
}

header h1 {
font-size: 16px;
text-align: right;
}

footer p.copyright {
float: left;
margin-top: 0px;
}

footer p.contact {
text-align: right;
}
```

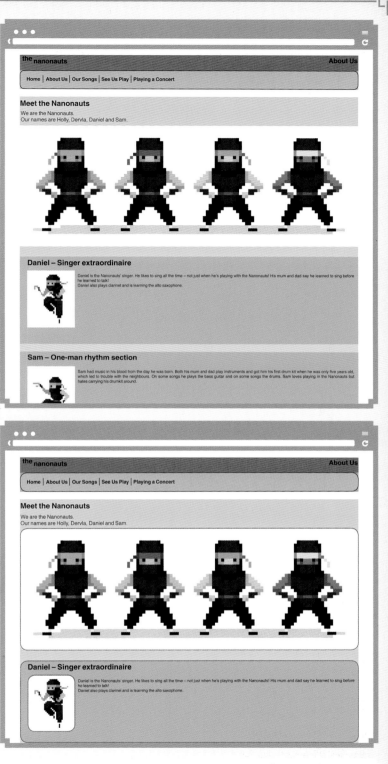

7. We'd now like to give the rounded borders to the body, section and image elements. To do this create a single rule which applies it to all the elements in one go. It looks like this:

```
body, section, img {
border: 2px solid Gray;
border-radius: 16px;
}
```

Notice the commas between the element names! Take the commas away and the elements to which the rule applies are completely different:

body, section, img   means 'apply this rule to **body** elements and **section** elements and **image** elements

body section img   means 'apply this rule to **img** elements which are inside **section** elements which are, in turn, inside **body** elements'

8. Now for the really interesting bit. At the moment, all of our structural elements are arranged one on top of the other, rather like a long ladder of elements. Try resizing your browser window to see what happens. Basically, the line length stretches, up to a maximum width of 1024px and then after that the right and left margins fill the window. But if we have a decent width available we could show the **aside** element to the right of the **article** element.

To do this we need to write a CSS rule that says: "when the screen is above a certain width, show the **article** and **aside** elements side by side" We do this using a special type of rule called a **media query.** This is our media query:

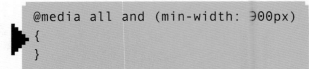

```
@media all and (min-width: 900px)
{
}
```

It begins with a statement which says when the query will be applied. **@media all and (min-width: 900px)**. We can break this short example down:

Notice that these three rules go inside the curly brackets of the media query. That's why the last rule has two brackets after it.

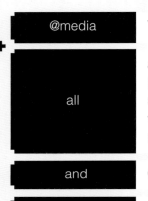

@media	This is a media query!
all	Applies to both the screen and physical printed pages (we could say 'print', if it only applied to printed versions of the page, or 'screen' to refer only to on-screen versions).
and	Connects the two.
(min-width: 900px)	This query will come into effect only when the browser window is wider than 900px.

```
@media all and (min-width: 900px)
{
article {
float: left;
width: 66%;
}
aside {
float: left;
padding-left: 24px;
width: 34%;
}
footer {
clear: both;
}
}
```

What these rules do is use the **float** property to position the **article** and the **aside** elements next to one another. By applying floats to both elements and then making their combined widths equal to 100% (66% for the article and 34% for the aside) we make them appear side-by-side when the window reaches 900 pixels in width. We add some padding to the left of the aside so that the borders don't bump up against each other when this happens.

Finally we add a **clear:both** rule to the footer element. This ends the floating elements and ensures that the footer appears in its normal position. If you don't add this rule, the footer floats to the right of the article – not the effect we're looking for!

THE RESULT!

You can easily swap the position of the article and aside elements, so that the aside appears on the left. To do this just replace **left** with **right** in the query. Like this:

```
@media all and (min-width:
900px) {
article {
float: right;
width: 66%;
}
aside {
float: right;
padding-right: 24px;
width: 34%;
}
footer {
clear: both;
}
}
```

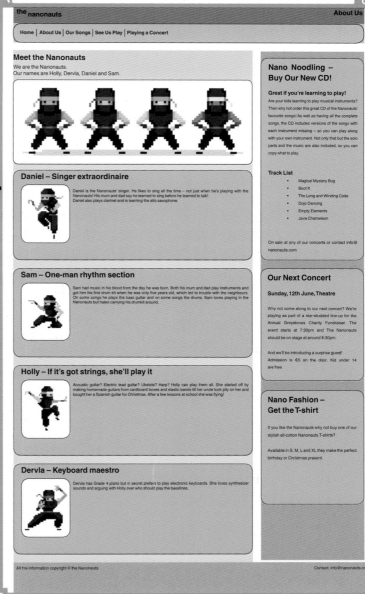

THINGS TO DO NEXT

Try to add a media query that makes the font smaller when the width is below 480 pixels.

9. Our page is just about finished. But lastly, we need to substitute the correct background colours for the structural elements and add the fancy page background into the **html** element. The colour rules are removed from the **header**, **aside** and **footer** elements, so they are the same colour as the **body**. The final stylesheet looks like this:

```css
/* set sizing to border box method */
html {
box-sizing: border-box;
}
*, *:before, *:after {
box-sizing: inherit;
}
/* set maximum and minimum widths for the body and centre within the viewport */
body {
background-color: Thistle;
font-family: sans-serif;
margin-left: auto;
margin-right: auto;
max-width: 1024px;
min-width: 256px;
padding-top: 8px;
padding-bottom: 24px;
padding-left: 24px;
padding-right: 24px;
}
/* add a fancy background */
html {
background: radial-gradient(circle, SkyBlue, SkyBlue 50%, LightCyan 50%, SkyBlue);
background-size: 8px 8px;
}
/* header */
header{
}
header p {
float: left;
font-size: 16px;
font-weight: bold;
margin-top: 0px;
}
header h1 {
font-size: 16px;
text-align: right;
}
/* the menu */
nav ul {
list-style-type: none;
background-color: #B577B5;
```

```css
border: 2px solid Black;
border-radius: 10px;
font-family: sans-serif;
font-weight: bold;
padding: 16px;
}
nav ul li {
display: inline;
border-right: 2px solid #111111;
padding-right: 8px;
padding-left: 8px;
}
nav ul li:last-child {
border-right: none;
}
nav ul li a {
text-decoration: none;
color: #111111;
}
nav li.selected{
color: #606060;
}
nav ul li a:hover {
text-decoration: underline;
}
/* biographies */
section {
background-color: #FFFFFF;
margin-bottom: 24px;
min-height: 320px;
padding-left: 24px;
padding-right: 24px;
}
/* the aside */
aside {
}
/* footer */
footer {
}
footer p.copyright {
float: left;
margin-top: 0px;
}
footer p.contact {
text-align: right;
}
```

```css
/* small images are set to 200px in height */
img.small {
float: left;
height: 200px;
margin-bottom: 24px;
margin-right: 24px;
}
/* medium images can be 50% of the container element's width, up to 360px */
img.medium {
max-width: 360px;
width: 50%;
}
/* large images are 100% of the container element's width */
img.large {
width: 100%;
}
/* add the same style of border to the elements which are to have borders */
body, section, img {
border: 2px solid #B1B1B1;
border-radius: 16px;
}
/* the bits that are specific to a wide viewport (over 56em) */
@media all and (min-width: 900px) {
article {
float: left;
width: 66%;
}
aside {
float: left;
padding-left: 24px;
width: 34%;
}
footer {
clear: both;
}
}
```

THE FINAL RESULT!

Meet the Nanonauts

We are the Nanonauts.

Our names are Holly, Dervla, Daniel and Sam.

Daniel – Singer extraordinaire

Dervla is the Nanonauts' singer. She likes to sing all the time – not just when she's playing with the Nanonauts! Her mum and dad say she learned to sing before she learned to talk! Dervla also plays the clarinet and is learning the alto saxophone.

Sam – One-man rhythm section

Sam had music in his blood from the day he was born. His dad says he was named after a famous folk musician (can you guess who?) but his says this is nonsense and he was named after a rabbit. On some songs he plays the bass guitar and on some songs the drums. Sam loves playing in the Nanonauts but hates carrying his drumkit around.

Holly – If it's got strings, she'll play it

Nano Noodling – Buy Our New CD!

Great if you're learning to play!

Are your kids learning to play musical instruments? Then why not order this great CD of the Nanonauts' favourite songs! As well as having all the complete songs, the CD includes versions of the songs with each instrument missing – so you can play along with your own instrument. Not only that but the solo parts and the music are also included, so you can copy what to play.

Track List

- Magical Mystery Bug
- Boot It
- The Long and Winding Code
- Dojo Dancing
- Empty Elements
- Java Chameleon

How to Buy

On sale at any of our concerts or contact info@nanonauts.com

Our Next Concert

Sunday, 12th June, Theatre

Why not come along to our next concert? We're playing as part of a star-studded line-up for the Annual Greystones Charity Fundraiser. The event starts at 7:30pm and The Nanonauts should be on stage at around 8:30pm.

And we'll be introducing a surprise guest! Admission is €5 on the door. Kids under 14 get in free.

FONTS

One of the best ways to change a page's appearance is to change the font. A font is a particular style of text. The fonts you choose for your page can have a huge effect on how the page appears.

If you want to pick a particular font then you'll need to use a **web font**. A web font is a special type of font that is downloaded along with the style sheet. Using a web font gives you more control than using a general name like `sans-serif` or `monospace`.

For example, if you choose monospace then the font that is used is different in Firefox and Chrome. However, if you choose a web font then it should appear the same in any up-to-date browser.

NINJA TIP

You must be online for web fonts to work. If you are looking at your web page but you don't have an internet connection you won't see the web fonts.

The easiest way to use a web font is to choose one from the Google Fonts page at https://www.google.com/fonts. Here you'll see a long list of fonts which you can choose from. Definitely more exciting than the boring default ones!

| Preview Text: | **Grumpy Wizards make toxic brew for the** | ▾ | ⌨ ▾ | Size: | **12px** ▾ | Sorting: | **Popularity** ▾ |

Normal 400

GRUMPY WIZARDS MAKE TOXIC BREW FOR THE EVIL QUEEN AND JACK.

Normal 400

Grumpy Wizards make toxic brew for the evil Queen and Jack.

Normal 400

Grumpy Wizards make toxic brew for the evil Queen and Jack.

Normal 400

GRUMPY WIZARDS MAKE TOXIC BREW FOR THE EVIL QUEEN AND JACK.

Once you found the font you're looking for, click the Quick Use icon.

The Quick Use page opens. In step 1 you can choose different styles, and in step 2, you can pick the characters that you'll need. This page gives you the information you'll need to add the web font to your site.

1. Choose the styles you want:

⊟ PT Sans Narrow

☑ Regular   Grumpy Wizards make toxic brew for the evil Queen and Jack.

☐ **Bold**   **Grumpy Wizards make toxic brew for the evil Queen and Jack.**

On this page, Step 3 and Step 4 are both very important! At Step 3 you'll see three tabs named 'Standard', '@import' and 'Javascript'. Click the '@import' tab. The code shown on the import tab is the code that you'll need to add to your stylesheet. It will look something like this:

Standard	@import	Javascript

3. Add this code to your website:

```
@import url(http://fonts.googleapis.com/css?family=PT+Sans+Narrow);
```

This line imports the font and makes it available for use in the stylesheet. You should add it as the first line in the stylesheet like this.

In the example above the **@import** statement will make a font called PT Sans Narrow available. But that's all – we haven't actually used the font anywhere. To do this we need to use the font in a rule within the stylesheet. That's where Step 4 comes in!

Step 4 tells us how to refer to the font in our stylesheet. It gives us a simple example of a declaration, something like the one below:

```
font-family: 'PT Sans Narrow',
sans-serif;
```

```
@import url(http://fonts.googleapis.com/
css?family=PT+Sans+Narrow);
body {
/* set sizing to border box method */
html {
box-sizing: border-box;
}
*, *:before, *:after {
box-sizing: inherit;
}
/* set maximum and minimum widths for the
body and centre within the viewport */
body {
font-family: sans-serif;
margin-left: auto;
margin-right: auto;
max-width: 1024px;
min-width: 256px;
padding-top: 8px;
```

89

PUTTING YOUR SITE ON THE WEB

So far you made a website that can only be seen on your own computer. But the whole point of a web page is that it's … well … on the web.

To do this you need to do two things:
- register a **domain name** (such as www.nanonauts.com)
- copy your site to a **web server** linked to the domain

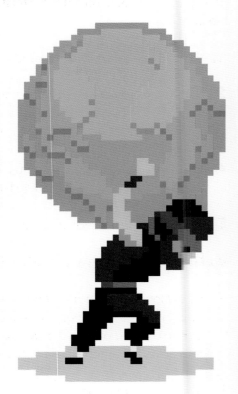

Then, when someone types your domain name into a web browser they are sent to the web server. A web server is just a computer which has been connected to the internet and which has been set up to send web pages to a computing device (phone, tablet, laptop and so on) that requests them.

Although setting all this up may sound a little complicated, it's actually made pretty easy because you can buy a **hosting package** from an internet service provider (ISP). A hosting package lets you rent some space on a web server for a small fee per month. Then, once you've chosen your package, all you need to do is pick your domain name and copy across your web pages. You do this using an **FTP program**.

USING AN FTP PROGRAM

An FTP, or 'file transfer protocol', program simply allows you to copy files between two computers which are connected to the internet. If you're copying files from your computer to the web server this is called **uploading**. If you're copying them from the web server to your computer, often referred to as the **local machine**. This is called **downloading**. You're probably already familiar with downloading: well this is your chance to do some uploading for a change! So how do you do it?

Once you've purchased your hosting package, you'll need to download and install an FTP program. A good free program is Filezilla which you can find at https://filezilla-project.org. Next you'll need the **IP address** of your webserver and a username and password. You normally get this information from the internet service provider when you purchase a hosting package. The IP address is a long number divided into four parts by full stops – for example, **66.175.209.200** – which allows the FTP program to find your web server.

NINJA TIP

URLs such as www.nanonauts.com are simply more user-friendly versions of IP addresses. In fact a URL simply tells a web browser to get files from a computer with a particular IP address.

Once you have the information you can start your FTP program and enter details of the computer you want to connect to. This is known as the 'host'. In Filezilla you do the following

NINJA TIP

The name of the web root folder may vary from one hosting package to another. Common names include:
- www
- wwwroot
- httpdocs
- public_html
- html
- public
- web

1. Choose File > Site Manager and click the New Site button.

2. In the left-hand window, give the site a name such as Nanonauts.

3. Enter the IP address of the server in the Host box.

4. If the service provider gave you a port number, you can enter this in the Port field. Usually you would leave this empty.

5. Change the logon type from Anonymous to Normal.

6. Enter the username and password.

7. Click Connect. After a second or two you should see details of the web server appear in the right-hand pane. When you connect to the web server it's important that you upload your files to the correct folder. This folder is known as the **web root**. The web root folder should always contain your `index.html` file and a copy of all the files and folders used to create your site on your local machine.

8. In the left-hand pane of Filezilla, copy across all the files in your local copy of the website to the webroot folder.

9. Select all the files and drag them across into the web root folder.

YOU'RE DONE!

Go to your web browser and type in the web address of your site. If all has gone well you should see your website! Congratulations, you now have your own site up and running on the web! Let your friends and family know!

BADGE UNLOCKED

WORLDWIDE!

CODE REFERENCE

As we've built our web pages we've been using a number of html elements. The table below contains a list of these elements. Mix-and-match as you need to build your pages!

Element	Meaning
a	A link. You put the page you want to link to in the **href** attribute.
body	The part of a web page which you can see in the browser.
em	Allows you to make important words or phrases stand out by appearing in sloping italic text.
h1	A major heading – usually used for the page's main title
h2	A secondary heading – used to divide up a long page into individual topics
h3	A minor heading – used to divide long topics up into smaller chunks
head	Contains information which the browser uses when working out how the page should be displayed.

Element	Meaning
html	All of your webpage must be inside a **html** element. A page can only have a single **html** element. The **html** element always contains a single **head** element followed by a single **body** element.
iframe	An **iframe** allows you to embed content from another site, such as YouTube or Google Maps inside your webpage. You say where to find the content by entering a URL inside the iframe's **src** attribute.
img	Allows you to display an image or picture. It's a good idea to give your image a **class** attribute with a value such as large, medium or small and then use the CSS to control the size of the image. The **src** attribute is used to locate the image.
li	An individual item in a list. **li** elements can occur inside **ul** and **ol** elements.
link	Provides the link to the CSS stylesheet which will be used to format the web page. The address of the stylesheet goes in the **href** attribute.

Element	Meaning
meta	Provides information to the browser which it uses to display the page correctly
ol	An ordered list. Used to create numbered lists. Each individual list item should be inside an **li** element.
p	A paragraph. Probably the most common element. If you want to create 'special' types of paragraphs (such as Tips or Notes) you can do so by using a **class** attribute.
strong	Allows you to make important words or phrases stand out by appearing in heavy bold text.
title	The title of the page that the browser will display in the page tab.
ul	An unordered list. Used to create bulleted lists and menus. Each individual list item should be inside an **li** element.

Attribute	Meaning
class	Any element can have a class attribute. The class attribute allows you to pick out elements which have a special purpose and format them in a distinctive way in your CSS.
href	Use within an **a** element to make a link. You put the address of the page you want to link to in the **href** attribute. Also used within the link element to identify the location of your CSS stylesheet.
id	A unique identification for a particular element. A particular **id** value must only occur once on a page.
src	Used within the **img** element to identify the source of the image (for example, **images/dervla.jpg**). Images usually end with a **.jpg** or **.png** file extension.

93

AFTERWORD

By now, you have your very own website up and running. Congratulations! It doesn't stop there, though. Code, and the computers that run it, is everywhere. It's in laptops, tablets, mobile phones and games consoles. It's in everything from car engines and refrigerators to electric toothbrushes!

The computer revolution didn't happen overnight. It took the cleverness and hard work of many people, working together and sharing their ideas.

A long time ago in Cork, Ireland, a man called George Boole had a really amazing idea: instead of having to use all sorts of different numbers to look at a problem, you could just use 0 and 1.

At around the same time a mathematician called Ada Lovelace was working with a mechanical genius called Charles Babbage, who was making a machine that could actually do maths. She wrote a set of commands that the machine would use to figure out maths problems.

In the 1930s, a man called John Vincent Atanasoff had a flash of brilliance, and created the first electronic computer using the work of Boole. It took instructions like the ones Ada Lovelace used in Babbage's machine.

The secret of this revolution is that to get a computer to do exactly what you want, to get it to do something totally new, all you need to know is how to speak to it. Because of coders like Ada Lovelace, we can photograph other galaxies using space telescopes powered by code. We can see a baby inside its mother's tummy using ultrasound powered by code. We can make incredible visions come true in the movies with code-powered animations and special effects.

Now you know the secret too, it's up to you what you do with it. I hope that whatever it is, you share the fun you have, and that whatever you build is cool!

— Bill Liao, CoderDojo Foundation